PARENTING
OCD

of related interest

Can I tell you about OCD?
A guide for friends, family and professionals
Amita Jassi
Foreword by Isobel Heyman
Part of the Can I tell you about...? series
ISBN 978 1 84905 381 5
eISBN 978 0 85700 736 0

Touch and Go Joe
An Adolescent's Experience of OCD
Joe Wells
Foreword by Isobel Heyman
ISBN 978 1 84310 391 2
eISBN 978 1 84642 489 2

Breaking Free from OCD
A CBT Guide for Young People and Their Families
Jo Derisley, Isobel Heyman, Sarah Robinson and Cynthia Turner
ISBN 978 1 84310 574 9
eISBN 978 1 84642 799 2

Starving the Anxiety Gremlin
A Cognitive Behavioural Therapy Workbook on
Anxiety Management for Young People
Kate Collins-Donnelly
ISBN 978 1 84905 341 9
eISBN 978 0 85700 672 1

A Practical Guide to Mental Health Problems in Children with Autistic Spectrum Disorder
It's not just their autism!
Khalid Karim, Alvina Ali and Michelle O'Reilly
ISBN 978 1 84905 323 5
eISBN 978 0 85700 697 4

A Short Introduction to Understanding and Supporting Children and Young People Who Self-Harm
Carol Fitzpatrick
Part of the JKP Short Introductions series
ISBN 978 1 84905 281 8
eISBN 978 0 85700 584 7

PARENTING
OCD

DOWN TO EARTH ADVICE FROM
ONE PARENT TO ANOTHER

Claire Sanders

Jessica Kingsley *Publishers*
London and Philadelphia

First published in 2015
by Jessica Kingsley Publishers
73 Collier Street
London N1 9BE, UK
and
400 Market Street, Suite 400
Philadelphia, PA 19106, USA

www.jkp.com

Library of Congress Cataloging in Publication Data
A CIP catalog record for this book is available from the Library of Congress

British Library Cataloguing in Publication Data
A CIP catalogue record for this book is available from the British Library

ISBN 978 1 84905 478 2
eISBN 978 0 85700 916 6

Printed and bound in Great Britain

*For my boogalloo who is the world's best little brother
and the light of my life...love you more.*

For the one who thinks he does nothing, but really does everything.

*And for the one who fights monsters and is my
hero. Thanks for letting me do this.*

Love you all x

ACKNOWLEDGEMENTS

With grateful thanks to Dr Amita Jassi and Mr D. Alavi –
for your help with this book and for everything else.

CONTENTS

About the Book

Chapter 1: OCD Warning Signs and Getting a Diagnosis

The early signs of OCD can be confusing. Our journey to diagnosis wasn't straightforward and there are some common pitfalls along the way that complicate the issue. In this chapter, I talk about how to recognise OCD, what to do if you suspect your child has OCD and the best ways to approach your doctor. I also share our own path to diagnosis and give you some tips on how to avoid the pitfalls so you can get help more easily.

Chapter 2: Therapy – Different Types, What Happens in Therapy and Beyond

What's the difference between CBT and ERP? How can talking about OCD, fight OCD? In this chapter, I talk about the types of therapy you will be offered, what they do and why they do it. Therapy can be a very stressful event, both for your child and for you. For us, therapy proved to be extremely difficult and required a huge amount of patience and persistence. I'll tell you my story about how we dealt with the problems therapy threw up, the ways I found to get around them and tips on how to get the best out of your child's therapy sessions.

Chapter 3: Medication

As a mother, I knew about Calpol and Vicks VapoRub. I could offer a little insight into nappy rash treatments too. Thrown into the world of medication for mental health reasons, I was lost. In this chapter I will share with you the different types of medication, how they work and why they are prescribed as well as our experience of taking medication when OCD says you shouldn't.

Chapter 4: When Initial Treatments Don't Help

Sometimes, therapy and medication don't produce the results you're looking for. It's times like these that you need to know what to do when it feels like you're out of options. In this chapter, I'll talk about how our son didn't respond, and what we did about it. I'll share some tips on how to recognise when things aren't working and the best ways I found to turn things around.

Chapter 5: School – Educating the Educators

OCD often affects your child's education. Mental health can be a difficult thing to explain, and you need your child's school to be fully on board; they can play a pivotol role in keeping some normality in your child's life. In this chapter I discuss how I handled issues to do with my son's education;

I talk about bullying and how to deal with tests and exams. You'll also learn how I handled it when my son could no longer attend school, how that affected us all and what we're doing about it.

Chapter 6: The Changing Nature of OCD

OCD can be like that fairground favourite game whack-a-mole, but the stakes are high! Symptoms come and go, they change and baffle you with the many guises of obsession. In this chapter I'll tell you about my son's changing OCD and why things can change. I'll also share with you my tips on how to deal with symptoms as they come and go.

Chapter 7: Tears, Tantrums and Other Outbursts

Anxiety, boredom, fear and frustration are all common emotions in a household that is affected by OCD. Panic attacks and high anxiety levels are everyday occurrences for a lot of us and they are hard to deal with. In this chapter, I talk about how anxiety affects our family, how my son's anxiety affects not just him, but all of us. I'll also share how living with my son's OCD affects my own anxiety levels, and leads to my own tantrums.

Chapter 8: The Rest of the Family

When your child has OCD, they are, of course, the person most dramatically affected. But the rest of us are affected, too. Everything changes and things aren't the way they used to be, aren't the way we planned for. Adapting to this new reality is a process the whole family has to go through and, in this chapter, I'll talk about how the process has affected our family, and how we are dealing with it. I'll share the things I've learned that help, and the things that make it worse.

Chapter 9: Things I've Learned to Help Me Cope

You may not be the one with OCD, but you are the one that has to deal with it. It takes a huge toll on a parent; it has definitely taken a huge toll on me. Through trial and error (mostly error), I've learned a lot about myself, how to stay strong and how to fight OCD when I feel I have nothing left. I'll share all this experience with you in this chapter.

Chapter 10: Common and Not So Common Obsessions and Compulsions

Although there has been a lot of exposure about OCD recently, not much is said about the stranger obsessions and compulsions that can pop up. We all know about hand washing and making things neat but what if OCD means becoming obsessed with God? Or with hurting other people? Or what if OCD wants you to confess to things you haven't done? What if the obsession is about sex? In this chapter we'll chat about the common, but not so widely known, obsessions that OCD can latch on to. Believe me, they may be shocking and hard to discuss, but I don't blush easy!

Chapter 11: Related Conditions – Other Nasties in OCD's Gang

Sometimes, OCD brings other members of its family along for the ride. In this chapter, I'll talk about other conditions that are sometimes found alongside OCD, or are a result of OCD. I'll talk to you about the warning signs and share with you the impact of OCD's nasty relatives on our lives.

Introduction

The thing about OCD is: if you haven't got it yourself, it's impossible to understand. There is no way any rationally thinking person can accept the beliefs OCD brings about. Trust me, I've tried, but I've had to accept that I will never understand why cracking your knuckle will prevent a car accident. Wouldn't it be great if it did, though? That bit I can understand. Imagine believing you can save lives by standing still, or counting, or jumping on the spot. No matter how inconvenient it is, you'd still do it, wouldn't you? You wouldn't think, 'Oh, I can't be bothered to count that, mum'll just have to die'.

The only thing you can try to understand is what is fuelling it. The rest is one long running battle, or a series of long battles as part of all-out war. For those of us not used to armed combat, it's hard. It's not just the actual OCD that becomes an issue for a parent or carer, though. You have to learn so quickly about treatments, therapy, medication, funding...you have to become a therapist. A live-in therapist. It's a rubbish job, I won't lie to you. You don't get breaks and the pay is awful. But someone's got to do it. If you've got to do it, here are some things I've learned along the way. Some may prove useful, some won't. Everyone's OCD is different, so pick out the bits that apply to you.

Firstly, a bit about me. Our son was diagnosed with OCD when he was ten. He'd started developing symptoms when he was six but things got gradually worse and worse as the years progressed. Our son is 13 at the moment and a lot has happened! Right now, he has been categorised as 'Extreme' and there isn't a moment of the day that isn't affected by OCD.

I don't have a medical degree; I'm not a trained therapist. I'm just the mother of a child with OCD who has a few battle scars. As the book goes along, I'll tell you more about our situation. If nothing else, I hope you'll feel less alone.

CHAPTER 1

OCD Warning Signs and Getting a Diagnosis

Firstly, it's really really important to say that if you have *any* suspicions that your child has OCD – *go to your doctor!*

What's OCD and what's just a kid liking something?

We have two children. One has OCD, one doesn't. One of our children is obsessed with superheroes. He can't get enough of them. Specifically, he *loves* Wolverine. Every conversation is peppered with amazing Wolverine facts, how Wolverine is stronger, faster, cleverer than any given thing. His room is covered in superhero pictures. Our other child is obsessed with germs. He is afraid of being in touch with anything he thinks may be contaminated. This includes other people and the outside world. He won't kiss and avoids physical contact even with family members.

So, which one has OCD? Of course, the one that's obsessed with germs. But they are both equally consumed by their obsession, so why is one healthy and the other not?

Our superhero-obsessed child, our youngest, loves Wolverine because he beats baddies. It's a quality he admires and wants to copy. It's not about being safe or protecting himself, it's about the kind of person he would like to be. So, it's not a bad thing. Also, he does like other things; he likes dinosaurs and chocolate and has a massive interest in sharks and tigers. He has a primary interest – Wolverine – and a range of lesser interests that balance the picture.

Our eldest child's obsession with germs is because he is afraid. He believes he could become contaminated and die, or vomit, which is worse. He avoids his fears at any cost, not going to school, not seeing friends. Not leaving the house. Not eating. None of that matters. What matters is…being clean. There is no balance. That's the difference.

These days, a lot of people know a little bit about OCD. Saying 'I'm a little bit OCD' has become a popular way of explaining a need to have things done 'our way'. We all have our 'quirks'. A lot of us like our cupboards to be tidy – it's efficient and prevents wasting time searching for things.

I myself like my tops in orderly piles of vests, short-sleeve casual, short-sleeve dressy, long-sleeve casual, long-sleeve … well, you get the picture. The difference is, if I found a short-sleeve casual top in my long-sleeve dressy pile, I'd just move it. I wouldn't feel that something dreadful was going to happen. I'd just be a bit irritated, at worst. I certainly wouldn't feel the need to 'cancel out' the mistake by performing rituals. I'd move the top and move on. That's because my need for my tops to be neatly piled is about me exerting my control over my environment. Someone with OCD's needs are more about their fear of having no control over their environment.

Most of us, if we were honest, have had that moment on the train platform where it occurs to us that we could push someone, or someone could push us, in front of the train. It's like a momentary urge to do it. So, we move back to the wall and think, 'Blimey, that was horrible'. It's more common than you think, that feeling that we may lose control and do something dreadful. It's true that the only thing that stops us doing these things is our conscience. Our morality.

People who have OCD fear that they will, momentarily, lose that control, and do something awful. That doesn't mean they are a risk of that. They're not violent, quite the opposite. They're just scared that they may lose control. That fear means that they are the people least likely to actually lose control, but that is little comfort to them. They feel really guilty about the thought, or impulse, often becoming convinced that they are a danger and avoiding situations where they may be a threat.

If your child does things to ward off danger that they feel they *must* do, get to the doctor. It may be nothing, but it may be something. Above all, trust your instincts.

Early signs

Our son was diagnosed with OCD when he was ten years old but, looking back, I can tell you the exact moment he had his first panic attack and we realised something was wrong; we just didn't know what it was at the time.

Our son was six when our youngest son was born, and I was prepared for some attention-seeking behaviour so when, one night, when our youngest son was about two weeks old, our eldest son came downstairs late at night with wild eyes, hyperventilating, flailing his arms around and screaming (literally, screaming) that he felt sick and thought he was going to throw up, I thought he was putting it on. I jumped up (as best I could two weeks after a Caesarean!) and rushed over to comfort him but he pushed me away, screaming, 'Don't touch me! Don't touch me! Help me! Please!'

We were absolutely shocked. He was crying and shaking, pacing up and down. We didn't know what to do. So, I firmly told him to calm down, and insisted that he sit down and stop it. After a while, he did calm down, and I thought I had handled it quite well. But, he did it again the next night, and the next, and the next. In fact, since that night, each and every night since then, for seven years now, he has had a panic attack where he feels sick, and is scared he will vomit. It doesn't seem to matter that he hasn't actually vomited since he was seven, he's still terrified every single night. The constant repetition does get to me. I mean, how many times can you tell someone the same thing? OCD has no logic though, you can't reason with it – normal reasoning does not apply. The sooner you accept that, the better off you'll be.

That was his only symptom back then, a fear of vomiting. It went on for so long that I took him to the doctor's and they checked him over, finding nothing wrong. The symptoms persisted, though, and so they referred him to a specialist who, after looking him over and running some tests, could also find nothing wrong. They thought it might be a reflux problem, so they prescribed antacids. They didn't work. He started to eat less and I remember having a chat with the lunchtime monitor at his school and asking her to keep an eye on him and let me know if he didn't eat.

After six visits over two years to the specialist, I began to suspect that the problem wasn't physical. It couldn't be, everything had been ruled out, but he was complaining more and more of persistent nausea. When he was nine, after two and a half years of this, I noticed that he was saying a little 'rhyme' to himself when he went to bed. He called it his 'Invisible' and it didn't make much sense. It started with his saying, 'I'm invisible. No one can see me. No one can hear me' and then went on a bit with words that really didn't make sense, ending with a long series of the words 'Shut, shut, shut' as he tapped himself in various places, his knees, his elbows, his head, his feet. It was as if he was casting a magical spell on himself, a protection of some kind, and had to cover his whole body with the 'magic'.

Then I noticed he was jumping onto his bed in a certain way, leaping onto it from a distance. I asked him why and he couldn't really explain, just said that he was scared to go right up to his bed. Now, when I was a little girl, I had a thing about a monster under my bed. To this day, I sleep with my feet firmly tucked into the duvet, as if a monster can't grab me if I'm covered with sheets! So, I thought it was something like that and he'd grow out of it.

I thought his 'Invisible' and him jumping on his bed were a childhood monster fear, so we got him a bed with drawers underneath that had no gaps between the bed and the floor. He still did it.

My mum took me to one side one day, and told me that she'd noticed he had a bit of a 'tic' in his eye. I had noticed it but, again, thought he would grow out of it. She also told me she'd noticed he kept saying the words 'I don't do that' out of the blue, another thing I'd noticed but decided to gloss over.

Looking back, I can't believe how dumb I was. How could I have thought that none of these things were related? At first, you don't, though. Kids do weird things all the time. That's part of the fun of being around kids – you never know what they're going to do, and they often do the least expected thing. Our son did unexpected things an awful lot!

Also, we'd had a bit of a bad time as a family when our son was eight. We lost my wonderful parents-in-law very close together and our son had been quite traumatised by that. Then, four months later, my mother was diagnosed with Motor Neurone Disease, which was a total shock and hugely traumatic. We were grieving and, yes, OK, I admit it, I took my eye off the ball. I wanted to believe that he would get over it in time.

I feel so dreadful about that. I should never have trivialised what he was going through. I should never have brushed it to one side. I was on auto pilot personally, getting through each day as my mother deteriorated very quickly. I didn't notice. I didn't want to notice. I will be ashamed of that for the rest of my days.

I did snap out of it, though. Our son was diagnosed in February of 2010, a year and a half after my in-laws passed away and a year before my own parents passed away, one week apart.

Now we look back on it, with the benefit of hindsight and better knowledge, we can see that our son was showing signs from the age of about two. It sounds incredible, doesn't it? He did, though. He had a 'thing' about the washing machine. He would sit on the floor, in front of the washing machine when it was turned off, for hours. He would get a tea towel and put it inside, then try to spin the drum. But it would never do what he wanted it to do so he would just scream and scream, then try again, and scream and scream…it went on all day, every day for over a year. So, all things considered, it was pretty obvious what was going on, it just took me some time to catch on.

I'm trying to forgive myself. If you were telling me this story, I would say to you, 'You had a lot going on, you're not a doctor! You did your best, and you got there in the end. We all make mistakes and yours are understandable' and I'd mean it, *do* mean it if you feel the same way. Tell that to my guilt. There's a reason people call a big thing 'the mother load'... every mother carries a huge sack of guilt, and that's mine.

Whatever your regrets are, forgive yourself. It's what you do now that counts. You're not judged by your mistakes, you're judged by how you fix them.

Going to the doctor

I hate to say it, but I haven't had a very good experience of doctors. Most of the ones I've seen are well meaning but not very well informed. It's a real shame and did have an effect on how quickly my son got treatment at the beginning. So, if you're really concerned, and you think your doctor hasn't understood you or didn't take you seriously, get a second opinion. Then, get a third opinion and keep going until you are satisfied.

It took three doctors to finally get our son referred. And then it was only because I insisted. Having finally realised that our son had something psychological going on, rather than physical, I plucked up the courage to take him to the doctor.

The first doctor told me to enrol our son in the Scouts. It would seem that, in her world, all he needed was to learn to tie knots and sing some rousing campfire medleys. She really said that! I knew it was nonsense but it made me feel quite embarrassed so I left it a while before going to a different doctor for another opinion.

The second doctor was shocking. She actually told me, in front of our son, that he was clearly feeling unloved and was inventing these problems as a way of getting my attention. Well, I was horrified. Given what we'd all been through, and how I felt I could've done more, I was just devastated. I knew that I showed my kids a lot of love and affection; whatever we'd been through didn't change that. I hugged them and told them I loved them all the time; it's a standing joke in our house! Blaming me as a mother was such a huge blow I can't describe how it felt.

So, I left it a while because I was worried: what if she was right? Mothers tend to blame themselves for everything at the best of times. Actually coming out and blaming me to my face was like a punch in the stomach.

Finally, our son was getting a lot worse so I decided to get organised. I started to make notes of what was happening, and when, in a little diary. Every time he did something strange, or I noticed something not quite right, I jotted it down. A picture began to emerge of the kind of things he was doing and how often. I made notes of his eating habits and things he told me about school and the truth of what was happening hit me. It was pretty obvious when you had it all in front of you, couldn't be argued with.

I put the main points from the diary into this list:

- *Distressing intrusive thoughts*

  Repeated thoughts of failure that interfere with ability to perform/concentrate at school, for example, 'If you answer this question, it'll be wrong and everyone will laugh.'

  Repeated instructions to prevent death of himself or family member (usually me), for example:

- ○ 'I must get to bottom of stairs before x or x will die'
- ○ 'I must hide x or x will die'
- ○ 'I must pick up stone or you will die' etc.
- ○ 'I cannot walk on cracks, lines or joins in flooring'
- ○ 'I cannot go upstairs alone.'

Scared of knives and heights.

Repeated urge to say 'I don't do that' to prevent whatever the intrusive thought is predicting. This happens in school and is noticed by other pupils.

- *Phobic fear of vomiting/illness*

Intrusive thoughts regularly predict vomiting. This provokes a serious anxiety attack.

Flees from people who are ill or who he fears are ill. He has locked himself in the bathroom in fear.

- *Ordering to the number four*

All sets of things, or anything that has to be counted, must be done to the number four. This interferes with his maths and all aspects of life.

- *Rituals*

Has a number of rituals that must be performed to prevent death, for example, he has a few rhymes he must say before sleeping, that also include a particular set of movements. He must do these until it feels 'right' and cannot sleep until this is achieved. Some nights he cannot achieve the 'right' feeling and an anxiety attack takes hold. The rhymes do not make sense.

- *Anxiety attacks*

  Regular, severe and occurring at any time. Can last all day. Sweating, shaking, pacing, wringing hands and won't allow physical contact. At least four times per week.

Armed with this, off I went to Doctor Number Three, showed it to her and just asked for a referral. And you know what? I got it, straight away. She immediately told me that she felt he had OCD and needed to see the local mental health team.

So, the moral of this unpleasant little episode is: don't give up. I hope your doctor is a lot more compassionate than ours, but if they're not, keep going back. Don't give up and don't blame yourself. It is *not* your fault.

I don't know how much time is spent at medical school learning about OCD. Don't be surprised if your doctor approaches OCD as a minor illness. Just move past them and go to see people who really do understand, because they are out there.

TIPS

★ Get a second opinion if you're not satisfied – and more if you need to.

★ Don't give up.

★ It is not your fault – there is nothing to be afraid or ashamed of.

★ Trust your instincts.

★ Keep a diary of symptoms – this will help your doctor understand the severity of the problem.

* Don't beat yourself up if it's taken a while to realise what's happening – you're not a doctor.

* Ask your child's school to help monitor symptoms while you're not there. How education is affected is vital to know.

* Speak to lunchtime staff if your child isn't eating at home. Your child may tell you that they ate their lunch at school, even if they didn't.

* If a symptom could have a physical cause – insist all possible causes are ruled out.

* Children can have quirks without it being OCD. Always check with your doctor if you are unsure.

Diagnosis – where to from there?

OK, so your child has been diagnosed with OCD. Probably, by the time you've got to this point, you aren't a bit surprised. But it's still a bit of a shock and you have to give yourself some time to process the information. I was relieved actually, because I felt getting a diagnosis meant that he would get the treatment and get better.

We were referred to our local CAMHS (Child and Adolescent Mental Health Services) and offered an assessment appointment with a psychiatrist. I was given the option of going without my son for the first assessment or taking him and, after talking to him, it was decided that I would go alone. You should do what you think is right but I have to say that going alone worked well. I had the chance to speak about the symptoms and my worries without my son being there, so I could be a lot more honest than I would have been. It's hard to talk about how I feel in front of our son. He gets so worried about me, and feels so guilty, plus, the more I show him I'm worried, the more worried he gets. So, I tend to downplay my concerns around him, to reassure him that everything's fine. He can't fight OCD when he's panicking so I have to be seen to be fairly relaxed about it all.

Whatever you decide to do, my advice is: take your list of the symptoms along with your bullet points of the things that are worrying you. There are often so many small things and you have a limited amount of time so your list will help you make sure you tell the psychiatrist all the things that are happening and they can build a clear picture of the situation very quickly. The clearer you can be the better. There's nothing worse than driving home and thinking, 'Oh! I forgot to tell them such and such!' Be clear, be honest and don't underestimate anything. What may seem like a small thing to you may be quite a telling thing to the professionals, so tell them everything, it'll really help things along.

Remember that you're also probably going to feel a bit emotional. It is hard to explain it out loud; every time I go through what my son's day is like, it's a shock. You're so involved in the day to day that you get used to a lot really easily. It's only when you say it out loud that you realise the impact of what's going on. So, your list will also help you communicate what needs to be told, leaving you free to have a good cry if you need one.

Our local psychiatrist was great. He saw immediately what the problem was and referred my son on for CBT sessions. He didn't judge me, or our son; he'd seen it all before and this is what he does for a living so he's not easily shocked!

Just so you have it, given below is the 'stepped-care' guideline from NICE (the National Institute for Health and Care Excellence) for OCD.[1] In the UK, it's NICE that draw up plans for how conditions should be treated; they lay down the protocols so that the medical field can be sure that they are doing all the right things at the right times. Most countries have their own versions of NICE and you should find your country's guidelines on the internet. It was a really important thing for me to know because, as things progressed, I was able to be prepared for the next step, or ask for the next step when it became appropriate, so I can't advise you strongly enough to educate yourself on how OCD is approached in your area of the world. Even if your part of the world doesn't have the same structure as here in the UK, this is still a good guide to the steps that should be taken to treat your child, as it was drawn up in consultation with one of the world's leading authorities on childhood OCD, who is based here in the UK. So, it has been put together by experts who know the best way to approach the condition and you should bear this in mind when seeking treatment for your child, wherever you are in the world.

Step 1

- individuals, public organisations, NHS
- awareness and recognition
- provide, seek and share information about OCD or body dysmorphic disorder (BDD) and its impact on individuals and families/carers.

---

1   Availiable at www.nice.org.uk/Guidance/CMG41/chapter/-3-a-stepped-care-approach-to-commissioning-high-quality-integrated-care-for-people-with-common, accessed 14 August 2014.

Step 2

- GP, practice nurses, school health advisors, health visitors, general health settings (including hospitals)
- CAMHS Tier 1
- recognition and assessment
- detect, educate, discuss treatment options, signpost voluntary support organisations, provide support to individuals/families/work/schools, or refer to any of the appropriate levels.

Step 3

- GP, primary care team, primary care mental health worker, family support team
- CAMHS Tier 1 and 2
- management and initial treatment of OCD or BDD
- assess and review, discuss options
- guided self-help (for OCD), CBT (including ERP), involve family/carers and consider involving school.

Step 4

- multidisciplinary care in primary or secondary care
- CAMHS Tier 2 and 3
- OCD or BDD with comorbidity or poor response to initial treatment
- assess and review, discuss options

- CBT (including ERP), then consider combined treatments of CBT (including ERP) with SSRI, alternative SSRI or Clomipramine.

Step 5

- multidisciplinary care with expertise in OCD/BDD
- CAMHS Tier 3 and 4
- OCD or BDD with significant comorbidity, or more severely impaired functioning and/or treatment resistance, partial response or relapse
- reassess, discuss options
- CBT (including ERP), then consider combined treatments of CBT (including ERP) with SSRI, alternative SSRI or Clomipramine. For young people consider referral to specialist services outside CAMHS if appropriate.

Step 6

- inpatient care or intensive treatment programmes
- CAMHS Tier 4
- OCD or BDD with risk to life, severe self-neglect or severe distress or disability
- reassess, discuss options, care coordination, SSRI or Clomipramine, CBT (including ERP), or combination of SSRI or Clomipramine and CBT (including ERP), augmentation strategies, consider admission or special living arrangements.

So, here in the UK, you'll start off at Step 1. Basically, this means your health provider should give you some information on OCD, how it affects the sufferer and the family. In our case, maybe that's what she was trying to do when she advised he join the Scouts? Hmmm...maybe not.

Moving on to Step 2 if Step 1 doesn't solve the problem, your health provider should talk to you some more about what's going on and what the treatment options are or refer you on to a mental health team for more specialist help.

Step 3 happens if they refer you in Step 2. At this point, you should be offered Cognitive Behavioural Therapy (CBT), including Exposure and Response Prevention (ERP) – don't worry, I explain what all that means in Chapter 2 which is about therapy. They should also talk to you about speaking to the school to get them on board with helping. You don't have to tell the school, though, it's up to you. I'll talk more about education in Chapter 5.

Then, if the CBT you are given in Step 3 doesn't help enough, we move on to Step 4. Each round of CBT is about three months, and they are unlikely to move up a step before it's completed. If things are bad enough, though, you should ask to move up. In Step 4, you will carry on with the therapy, and you should have a review with the psychiatrist where you will consider medication. We'll talk about that in the next chapter. If medication is prescribed, it will be three months before you get another review.

If another three months go by and things are not improving, you should move up to Step 5. Here you carry on with the CBT and they will play around with the medication, adding another or changing for another one. Again, it's three months to see if this helps or not. But, if things are getting worse, this is the point where you will talk about being referred to a specialist service. Step 5 doesn't have a length of time; if you get referred on to a specialist centre, they will stay with you until things have improved. I'll tell you about specialist centres in Chapter 4.

In the hugely unlikely event you get through Step 5 without success, we have Step 6. This is the same as Step 5 except they may consider admitting to hospital. It really is very rare that this happens.

Unfortunately, I have to tell you that hospitalisation did happen for my son, but, really, it was quite a positive experience, all things considered. The main reason he was admitted was that the problems with his eating became so bad that he risked becoming physically ill if they carried on. Also, although he had made significant progress, it was too slow and he was missing out on his entire childhood. Something needed to be done to give him back his life, and I had to accept that I couldn't do it.

I stress, again, that this isn't a common thing to happen, although it can happen in the most severe cases. Children will always respond better if they are at home and normal life continues, so please don't take our situation as the way it goes. Sometimes, it is the way it goes, but more often than not, it goes a lot better than our example.

Sometimes, and if it happens it's a good thing, your health provider will just refer you immediately for therapy. It's important to carefully find the right approach for each individual. It is really important that you give each step a chance to work. Jumping straight in and insisting on medication from the outset may not be the best course of action. If you've found the right therapist, you should be able to trust their judgement. Try not to allow your alarm as a parent to cloud the issue. Professionals treat this condition all the time and you should let them do their job. That said, you should use the guidelines to help you know when enough time has been given, so that you can make good decisions at the right times.

I've found that having a structured approach to treatment really works. Although our son's OCD hasn't responded, don't let that put you off. OCD is such a slippery character that you need a game plan to help you stay on the right tracks, and not get diverted by symptoms.

In the early days of our son's OCD, I felt as if everything was out of control. So much was changing, all our lives were affected and nothing seemed to make any difference. It felt like this would go on forever, a never-ending cycle of therapy sessions that didn't help. I have been so afraid for our son. I hate using the words 'I need to be in control' because it reminds me so much of the root of so many of my son's problems, but I did need to be in control of the situation. It was either me in control, or OCD. So, having a game plan, giving each stage a fair time period to see if it worked, having a cut-off point where we would talk about next steps if it didn't when that time period was up, gave me back a sense of order, a feeling of control. I don't know how much that's helped my son, but it's really helped me.

For those of you reading this outside of the UK, I understand that your medical system may be vastly different to ours. We have a National Health Service which means that all of our treatment is free, well, I say free, the taxpayer pays for it. We are truly lucky to have the excellent service we receive and I'm sure we are the envy of many people around the world.

If your child's treatment needs to be funded by your medical insurance, I think this could be a benefit. It means you get to 'shop around' for your therapist and is why I've included the UK's guidelines, as it will help you select a therapist with a structure already in mind, and to help you recognise a therapist who understands OCD when you meet them.

TIPS

* Take your symptoms diary with you to each appointment – or write a list of your concerns.

* Be as clear as possible with your psychiatrist.

* If you aren't offered the choice to go alone or with your child for a first appointment – ask for it.

* Ask the psychiatrist to explain what treatment they are prescribing.

* Don't be scared to ask questions.

* Give each new treatment a fair chance to work. OCD can take time to respond, and often gets worse before it gets better.

* Have a game plan in your head to help you manage your feelings of fear.

* If you're choosing a therapist for your child, discuss your game plan with them to ensure that they agree with the recommended approach.

CHAPTER 2

Therapy

Different Types, What Happens in Therapy and Beyond

The medical field love abbreviations. The number of times I've sounded a million times more knowledgeable than I am, just because I spoke in a series of letters, makes me laugh! If ever you want a doctor to take you seriously, learn the abbreviations. There's nothing like a perfectly delivered, 'But bi-monthly CBT is proving ineffective, even given the ERP element. We should progress to Step 4 and consider an SSRI.' The look on their faces is a beautiful thing! All I've said is, 'Therapy's not working, let's try medication' – but it's all in the delivery.

Here are a few abbreviations that you need to know. CBT stands for Cognitive Behavioural Therapy. CBT is a talking and doing therapy. In CBT of for OCD, the focus is to help young people and families understand how OCD and anxiety work and the use the main tool called Exposure and Response Prevention (ERP) tasks to help them fight OCD. ERP is when the child is asked to face the fear (exposure) and fight the action/doing the ritual (response prevention).

Basically, it's a bit like the way you get over a phobia of spiders. First, you'd think about a spider. Then, you might look at a picture of a spider. Then, you'd sit in a room with a spider in a glass box at the other end. And so on, until, finally, you're sitting with a spider in your hand and you're OK with that. The idea is that the more you are exposed to something, the more used to it you get, and the less afraid.

So, in an ERP session for OCD, they will make a list of your fears and decide which are the worst, drawing up a scale of seriousness that they call the hierarchy. Most therapists usually start off with the least scary ones and then they work their way up the list. So, if, for example, they're working on a need to wash your hands, you'll work out how many times a day you wash your hands. Let's say it's 30 times. For the first week, they'll ask you to drop one hand wash or so. Once you're used to that and not feeling as anxious, you'll drop more etc.

It is brutal at first, but gets easier as you go along. The more children with OCD face their fears, the less afraid they become.

It is important that you know that, although the therapist will be leading the CBT or ERP sessions, you will be the one following through at home. This can be really tough because your child generally feels more able to tell you to get lost! They can experience severe anxiety when they don't perform their rituals, I don't need to tell you that, so working on supporting them when the urge to perform a ritual is overwhelming and they're very afraid is hard.

Be prepared to be tired, I mean down to your bones knackered. Also, it is hard on you emotionally. Watching your child in that state and not stepping in and making it better is a bit like torture but you *must* resist the urge to reassure them.

I look at it the way I did when I was training my toddlers to sleep in their own beds and not crawl into mine at midnight. *Supernanny*, a reality show for parents having a difficult time with their children, taught me that once I'd told them to stay where they are, I have to stick with it. If I crumble and let them get into my bed again, even once, it's game over. Because I have just taught them that all they have to do is keep screaming and I'll give up.

OCD is like that in my head. If I say, 'You will eat that cheese', I have to be prepared to make him sit for hours if necessary, until it's eaten. If I say eat it and then let him not eat it, what are the chances he will eat it tomorrow?

So, if your child is anxious, feels that something's wrong, tell them *once* that it's OK. Then, no matter how often they beg you to tell them again, just keep reminding them that you've already answered that question, in a calm, relaxed voice. Don't let your voice sound stressed or upset (even though you're bound to be feeling both of those things) because the more confident you are, the more confidence they have. Or if they're anxious because you won't let them wash their hands, don't cave and let them have a quick wash, or give them a wet wipe (it still counts!). If you do that, you've made it harder tomorrow.

During therapy I've seen some of the lowest points of my life. Our son had a maddening tendency to lie during therapy. He'd be in all sorts of trouble on the way there, doing about 20 rituals to prevent God knows what happening, then he'd sit with a calm smile on his face during the session, agreeing with everything the therapist said! To the point that the therapist actually thought he was getting better when the truth was, he was twice as bad!

Fortunately (in some ways), he lost the ability to control his anxiety and one day melted down completely in therapy, screaming and shouting to get out. I've never seen a therapist so surprised! Awful though it was, I was so relieved; at least now they could see what was really happening, and things moved more quickly treatment-wise from that point.

Be prepared for that to happen, especially if your child is concerned with pleasing others. It's really hard for them to tell the therapist that they don't agree. A lot of the CBT therapy is trying to draw the child out and get them talking, so to do this, a therapist may ask questions like 'I think you could stop washing your hands, do you?' Whilst we want our child to be positive, if that's not what they believe, they should tell the truth, and say 'no'; this allows the therapist to then ask why not and try to get that opinion challenged and changed. It makes things a lot harder when they tell the therapist what they want to hear.

A lot of our breakthroughs have come when my son was unable to hide how he was feeling, no matter how much he wanted to. It's like going to the doctor with stomach ache and not telling the doctor that your stomach hurts. There's no way he can fix what he doesn't know about.

According to NICE guidelines (in the UK), each round of therapy should include CBT and ERP and last three months. You should get a review with the psychiatrist at the end of each round, where you will all sit down and discuss progress and next steps.

Factors in the success of ERP therapy

I've worked out that, over the years, we've had around 250 hours of therapy. That's a lot of hours. Seriously, four years of one hour per week, and that's without the follow-through at home which is 24 hours per day, seven days per week. I don't even want to add all that time up, it's too depressing.

Hours and hours spent going round and round, and feeling like we're getting nowhere. Different therapists all doing their level best to help our son, us doing our level best to help our son, nothing helping our son.

CBT with ERP works. It's helped thousands of people; the evidence is impossible to argue with and I don't argue with it. The deciding factor of the success rate, though, is the willingness of the OCD sufferer to do the tasks. Now, I don't mean willingness as in they may be too lazy; often the sufferer really wants to get better but the thought of defying OCD or not doing their rituals is just too terrifying.

That's why it's best to begin with rituals that aren't too scary. There will be rituals for every OCD sufferer that are less scary to stop doing. I don't mean they're not at all scary, but they're not as scary as some of the others. If you start with those, you give your child a chance to prove to themselves that they can do it. They begin to believe that OCD is lying; gradually their confidence in their own ability to withstand their anxiety increases and they are prepared to move on to the more difficult rituals.

The very first thing to do, though, is to help your child understand what anxiety is, why it makes their bodies feel the way it does, and why our bodies do this. Education is vital to help take the fear out of the situation and nobody should go into an ERP task without solid knowledge of how anxiety works. So, here's the lowdown on anxiety as it's been explained to me.

We are genetically programmed to experience anxiety. Since we were cavemen, we've relied on our ability to react to extreme danger in a way that gives us a better chance of surviving. It's called 'Fight or Flight'. The 'Fight or Flight' response is not something we can control. We're hard-wired that way, and we need that reaction; it keeps us safe when there is genuine danger. We are flooded with adrenaline so that we are stronger to fight the danger, or faster to run away from it. The problem with OCD is: that natural reaction is provoked over any little thing, real or imagined. We were told that it's like your car alarm. Have you ever had that one annoying car in the street whose alarm goes off every time the wind blows, or someone walks past it? (We had to admit that we were that annoying car in the street for a while.) An OCD sufferer's brain has the same problem. The alarm is there for a good reason; it's just over-sensitive and keeps going off when it shouldn't. So, you get all the symptoms of being in mortal danger, without the actual danger. It's very hard to ignore, it's impossible to ignore actually. You have no control over it.

The physical symptoms of this adrenaline flood can be shaking, sweating, racing heartbeat, breathing more quickly and headaches. It can make us feel quite nauseous, too, as our body automatically diverts essential blood flow away from less important functions like our stomach and to our heart and lungs to be used as fuel. The rapid breathing can make you very dizzy as you breathe too quickly to exhale all of the built up carbon dioxide from your lungs. It can be very scary, and it is certainly extremely unpleasant. Avoiding these anxiety symptoms is the reason OCD exists. If the sufferer is less afraid of how anxiety can make them feel, they are less likely to enter into rituals to control it, or avoid situations that can trigger it.

None of the symptoms are permanent, though. That's the most important thing to know. None of them will cause any permanent damage. As the anxiety passes, so, too, do the symptoms. Leaving us shaken and drained but entirely unscathed.

Understanding this natural process is very important. It doesn't mean you're dying, or going to have a heart attack, nothing bad will happen to you and it will pass. Your body is doing exactly what it was designed to do, it's just doing it over the wrong things.

Only when your child understands this can they be prepared to actually make themselves experience it in an ERP task. The preparation is everything.

TIPS

★   Be open with your child's therapist.

★   Be prepared for therapy to be hard.

★   Ask about your child's therapist's qualifications.

★   If you don't bond with your child's therapist – ask about the possibility of a change.

★   Give therapy a chance – it takes time.

★   Learn about anxiety, understand the physical symptoms.

★   Be prepared for your child to be uncooperative.

★   Encourage your child to be honest – even if it feels like resistance.

★ Look after yourself – it's hard work.

★ Never reassure more than once.

★ Don't be afraid of anxiety – it won't hurt them and it will pass.

★ The more your child faces their fears – the more fears they will face – every time they do it is a victory so celebrate!

CHAPTER 3
Medication

When the psychiatrist raised the question of medication with me, he spoke to me as if I would be really reluctant and worried about it. Maybe I should have been, but I wasn't. By that point, I wanted something to make my son better and if a tablet a day could achieve that, bring it on!

There are two main categories of medication used to treat OCD: SSRIs and tricyclics. They both work on the serotonin levels in the brain. It is thought that OCD has something to do with serotonin levels in the brain. Quite a few mental health problems are the result of an imbalance of serotonin.

Serotonin is a neurotransmitter. Our body communicates with the brain through our nerves and our nerves are made of nerve cells. It looks a bit like a bath plug chain, with the links and balls. Anyway, between each ball is a gap. Somehow, the message needs to jump across the gap if it is going to reach the brain. The body uses serotonin to get the messages across the gap. The theory on OCD and serotonin is that there is not enough serotonin to get the messages across the gaps properly. This results in messages not being received clearly.

SSRIs and tricyclics do the same thing, but in different ways. They are used to treat mood disorders, such as depression, bipolar disorder, OCD and others. When I learned that, I was a bit confused that OCD was being treated as a mood disorder, as it's not like people with OCD have manic highs or lows, but it turns out that these medications block the serotonin transporter which makes more neurotransmitters grow outside the cell. When that happens, there are more neurotransmitters to carry a message, and the messages get through more clearly.

I look at it like this. Someone without OCD thinks, 'That knife is sharp, be careful'. So, they are careful when they use the knife. The message has got through exactly as it was supposed to.

Someone with OCD thinks, 'That knife is sharp, be careful'. As the message is sent along the line to the part of the brain that makes sure you're careful, a bit of Chinese Whispers happens. The first neurotransmitter says, 'That knife's sharp, be careful, pass it on'; the second one says, 'That knife's sharp, be careful you don't hurt yourself, pass it on'; the third says, 'That knife's sharp, you could hurt yourself, pass it on'; and by the time you get to the brain, it hears, *'sharp knife! You're going to hurt yourself!'* The person with OCD gets a flood of panic because they are now being told that there is significant danger if they hold this knife and they should put it down immediately and run! And the same is true for germs and anything else. It's just Chinese Whispers.

Both SSRIs and tricyclics work on stopping Chinese Whispers, helping the neurotransmitters to repeat the message exactly the same as the one before until it reaches the brain.

SSRIs

More abbreviations for you to learn: SSRI stands for Selective Serotonin Reuptake Inhibitor. They are a type of antidepressant that has been found to work quite well for OCD. The main ones prescribed for OCD are:

• Sertraline

• Citalopram.

They both work on the serotonin levels in the brain. Unfortunately, as with all medication, they can have side effects. The most common ones are:

• nausea

• insomnia

• diarrhea

• dry mouth

• somnolence (being tired)

• dizziness

• tremor.

And there are some other sexual problems with erections and loss of libido that can occur but, as I'm writing this as a mother, I'll stick my fingers in my ears and shout *la la la* at the top of my voice.

An important point: it will take at least two weeks before the level of medication in the bloodstream is high enough to make a difference, so don't expect changes quickly.

Tricyclics

Tricyclics have been used since the 1950s. If a SSRI doesn't work, the standard procedure is to try a tricyclic to see if that makes a difference. The usual tricyclic prescribed is Clomipramine. They're called tricyclics because they're made up of three rings of atoms – 'tri' meaning three.

The medical world moved from tricyclics to SSRIs because there can be more side effects with the older tricyclic drugs. However, if you leave the side effects aside, Tricyclics have been found to be slightly more effective in the treatment of OCD so it's not a bad thing to try one if SSRIs aren't working.

The most common side effects are:

- drowsiness
- dry mouth
- sweating
- nausea/vomiting
- constipation
- blurred vision
- difficulty passing urine
- changes in appetite
- headache
- dizziness
- weight gain/loss.

And, again, quite a lot of sexual problems with libido and erections.

Other medications that may be used

In certain cases, it may be helpful to prescribe a type of medication called an antipsychotic. That word – psychotic – really shocked me when it was first mentioned. It carries so many preconceptions of mental illness, doesn't it? Calling someone a 'psycho' is a common way of describing someone dangerous, out of control, mad. So, suggesting that our son should take an antipsychotic felt as if he was being classified as amongst that group. It wasn't nice.

But, with the benefit of more experience I've come to realise that the word 'psychotic' is used incorrectly. An antipsychotic drug is used to control anxiety, and it is very useful in controlling unwanted thoughts, kind of normalizing the way the brain processes thoughts. In OCD, that can be a very useful tool, so please don't be too alarmed if your child is prescribed this treatment.

Antipsychotics work by affecting the neurotransmitters in our brains, mainly dopamine. We've talked about neurotransmitters earlier; these are the little guys responsible for how our brain cells communicate with each other, things like how important or interesting we find something, how satisfied we feel or how motivated. Dopamine is also involved in controlling muscle movement. It is thought that, if the dopamine system is over-active, that can make us hallucinate, become delusional and have distressing thoughts. Sound familiar? With that in mind then, it now feels to me like a good, solid option. I just wish they were called something else.

In the past, antipsychotics were known as tranquillisers and the 'typical' range of them does have a tranquillising effect, but the newer drugs, called 'atypical', are not designed to make you sleepy or calmer. They shouldn't really affect your day-to-day function, so they aren't like Valium or sleeping tablets at all.

For us, of course, it wasn't straightforward and, when I had finally gotten my head around our son taking an antipsychotic, it emerged that he's allergic to them. We just can't seem to catch a break, can we? He broke out in a very nasty rash, red and itchy, so we had to stop him taking them. Fortunately, that's very uncommon; the side effects are actually quite mild. Except in our son's case, which really shouldn't surprise me in the least.

Our experience of medication

What is a tablet? It's a lump of chemicals. So, how do you convince an OCD sufferer who is terrified of chemicals that it's a good idea to swallow some?

Getting my son to take medication has proved to be so difficult. In fact, he point blank refused to take the tricyclic at all. He did take Sertraline but it didn't really help. Don't let that put you off because I know that it does help most people, we were just unlucky enough to be in the minority of sufferers that it didn't help.

On the positive side, he didn't experience any of the side effects either, which I was very relieved by. My son is absolutely terrified of vomiting and sleeping, so being told that the medication could make him nauseous and sleepy made me quite nervous!

Our three months on Sertraline started off really well. I was so relieved that we were trying something new, I suppose I got my hopes up. He took a low dose at first for the first four weeks, then, when that wasn't working, they increased it, and then increased it again, and again until he was taking the maximum dose and we had to admit defeat.

Every morning was a battle to get him to take it. Poor little thing, he was so scared, and I felt awful putting him through it but I knew it was the right thing to do. It hurts more than you'd think to have your child look at you as if you're poisoning them, but that's how he felt about it.

By the time we moved over to Citalopram, his fear of medication was getting a lot stronger but I, trusting fool that I am, continued to bring him his breakfast, a drink and his tablet in the morning and leave him to it. It was only when I was looking for a lost remote control in his room that I opened his bottom drawer and there they were, about four weeks' worth of tablets stashed away. I'll never forget the physical feeling of being winded that I felt when I saw that. He'd also stashed all the toast and breakfast bars I'd been bringing him.

For some reason I found that absolutely devastating. He was 11 by this point and we'd always been so close, it was a physical pain to realise that he'd been lying to me every day for a month, even though I knew it was because he was scared, not naughty. The knowledge that he was in such a state that he was hiding things from me changed our relationship and the trust that we had between us. Until then, I'd always assumed he'd tell me if something was wrong. That day I learned that his OCD is stronger than his bond with me, and I would have to fight like a tiger to get him back. I wasn't in charge anymore.

But, the trust was gone and the days of me standing over him, watching him take his tablet, making him open his mouth after he'd swallowed to check it was gone and insisting that he eats in front of me, began.

I hate not being able to trust him, it's the bit I miss the most. I know that as kids age, there are things that they keep from their parents. We've all done it. But, big things, important things, things that really affect your life, you just imagine that they'll always be shared. For a mother who's always been really open and talked to her kids about anything to realise that there are things he can't tell you... I felt I'd lost him and it hurt.

So, Citalopram didn't help and his psychiatrist prescribed a tricyclic. Unfortunately, he described the side effects to my son and that was that.

I know that ethically it's right to explain to a patient what the possible side effects of a medication could be. But, I can't help thinking that my son was not making good decisions for himself and that information led him to making a very bad decision, and not taking them. When my son said to the psychiatrist that he wouldn't take them, the psychiatrist advised me that I could maybe hide them in food so he wouldn't know. A great idea, but not so great that the 'secret' was discussed in front of my horror-stricken child.

Considering that we already had huge eating problems (he won't eat dairy and a range of other things, anything really, because he's afraid the food is 'contaminated'), it was a mistake to suggest that there may be something in his food that may make him vomit. It led to my son refusing to eat for a while, and the only way he could be persuaded to eat was if he watched me prepare the food.

I know that it is a cardinal sin to give in to his fears like that but, when your child isn't eating, and he really will happily go days without food if I let him, you feel over a barrel. The most important thing is to get as much nutrition into him as possible. Every mealtime is a battle to get him to eat, so I'm not really giving in to OCD; if I was, I'd let him starve. I've tried that, by the way, and he did starve. He didn't eat for four days and would have carried on if I hadn't jumped in. I chose my battleground, and it's food.

TIPS

* If your child is worried about taking medication, be prepared to monitor them taking it.

* OCD will win some battles – it's the war you need to focus on.

* Talk to your psychiatrist alone about discussing side effects with your child.

* Medication takes at least two weeks to begin working and longer to be at full speed – be patient.

* Don't lose heart if medication doesn't work at first – ask for alternative plans.

* If your child hates you because you're making them take tablets – trust the bond you have with them. They don't really hate you, OCD hates you and that's OK, I'm sure the feeling is mutual!

* Choose your battlegrounds – symptoms that risk physical health are your priority. Mental health must take a back seat if physical health is in jeopardy. So, if you have to give in to OCD to preserve physical health, you're doing the right thing. You can pick up the battle with OCD once that threat has passed.

CHAPTER 4

When Initial Treatments Don't Help

The success rate of Steps 1–4 is high. It's very unusual for them not to result in a good recovery or, at least, significant progress. Sometimes, very occasionally, though…you have to move to Step 5 because things aren't getting any better. My son was one of those children. For reasons we don't completely understand, he just got worse, despite huge efforts by our local CAMHS.

He had therapy every other week for a year, he was prescribed three different courses of medication but, he just got worse and worse. When we started therapy, in May, he was attending school. He wasn't really participating in classes, though, he spent most of his day in the support worker's office and was very, very anxious but he was going every day. He was sleeping at night, too and, he was eating.

As I suggested in Chapter 1, I wrote a list of the things that were worrying me about my son for my first meeting with his psychiatrist in February. The list I took is given on pp.24–26.

So, things were worrying and, at the time, I thought things were pretty bad. If only I had known what was coming!

After about six weeks of therapy, he started to worry about eating. I noticed that his appetite was getting less and less and that he wouldn't eat dairy. He started to lose weight and finally confessed that he was scared that the food was off or dirty and could make him vomit. It was at about the same time that he started to develop problems sleeping. He became really scared of sleep, convinced that he would die in his sleep or that something bad would happen and he wouldn't wake up in time to stop it. He got more and more tired, thinner and thinner. I tell you, it was terrible to watch. That was when he was first prescribed an SSRI and, as I said in the previous chapter, he did take that course.

At the end of July, he was due to break up from school and move on to senior school. I knew that was going to be difficult for him, so I met with the new school in advance to prepare them, and to try and smooth the way for transition. Again, I took in a list of my son's symptoms to help them understand the kind of issues he faces during the day and to help them figure out a way to deal with the problems.

This is the list I took. You'll notice it's got a bit longer!

Obsessions:
- fears of harming himself or others
- fears of odd numbers
- fear of 'the middle'
- fear of contamination through food or liquid
- fear of illness
- fear of germs
- repeated intrusive thoughts.

Compulsions which he thinks help him 'manage' these obsessions:

- avoiding 'the middle'
- re-organising objects
- avoiding knives and other sharp objects
- avoiding open windows and heights
- restricting food and drink
- avoiding sleeping
- avoiding odd numbers in maths or in paper question form
- avoiding 'odd number' stairs
- repeating words read aloud 'incorrectly' until they are 'right'
- repeatedly correcting words written 'incorrectly' until they are 'right'
- staying still and not blinking for periods of time
- avoiding cracks, joins or patterns in flooring
- procrastination when given a deadline
- frequent mental compulsions such as counting etc.

Things that make it worse:

- tests
- bullying
- stress
- change
- being alone
- guilt.

How this affects his day at school:

- lateness for class due to being 'stuck' in a ritual
- difficulty concentrating in class due to intrusive thoughts
- anxiety in crowds
- anxiety at mealtimes
- difficulty with handwriting
- difficulty with maths
- difficulty with peers
- low self-esteem
- difficulty with deadlines
- tiredness in class due to exhaustion from symptoms and lack of sleep.

So, things were going downhill very fast!

The school tried to understand, but, really, you should have seen their faces! I tried to prepare them, but nothing did! I'll go more into the education side of things later, and we'll talk in more detail about preparing school and getting the best out of them.

Now, below is the same list but I've added the extra things that popped up in about eight months:

Obsessions:

- fears of harming himself or others
- fears of odd numbers
- fear of 'the middle'
- fear of contamination through food or liquid
- fear of illness

- fear of germs
- repeated intrusive thoughts
- agorophobia
- fear of clowns
- fear of fire
- fear of the stairs
- fear of drowning
- fear of dying.

Compulsions which he thinks help him 'manage' these obsessions:
- avoiding 'the middle'
- re-organising objects
- avoiding knives and other sharp objects
- avoiding open windows and heights
- restricting food and drink
- avoiding sleeping
- avoiding odd numbers in maths or in paper question form
- avoiding 'odd number' stairs
- repeating words read aloud 'incorrectly' until they are 'right'
- repeatedly correcting words written 'incorrectly' until they are 'right'
- staying still and not blinking for periods of time
- avoiding cracks, joins or patterns in flooring
- procrastination when given a deadline
- frequent mental compulsions such as counting etc.

- hiding in the cupboard
- opening and closing doors
- cleaning his room
- washing his hands
- washing his body
- hurting himself
- not leaving his room and urinating in a bucket at night
- restricting defecation
- not putting things back where they came from in the kitchen
- making the sign of the cross
- pacing around bedroom
- cannot lie on, or touch, his bed – sleeps on the floor
- won't bath as he feels he would be 'sitting in his own filth'
- sometimes can't leave his bedroom
- avoids the garage where tools are kept
- objects must be placed in a particular order
- practising handwriting to perfect it (it's never perfect)
- counting during the advert breaks on TV
- pulling out hairs
- throwing his head back violently
- staying still; freezing in mid motion, sometimes in dangerous places
- refusing to leave the house
- doesn't see friends, due to fears they have germs

- will only brush teeth with new toothbrush
- won't allow parents to kiss him
- won't sit on chairs others have sat on
- refuses to take any medication, even vitamin supplements
- tapping objects
- jumping on the spot.

He was going downhill faster than I could keep up, a constantly changing picture that got no prettier with time. This is the last list I wrote before I gave up. It got so long, there was no way of keeping up with it. Things came and went, new rituals popping up, old ones dying down. For every ritual that died down, two popped up, so I stopped. It was just too depressing and I didn't need to anymore.

My son refused to believe he has OCD. He didn't know exactly what was going on, but he insisted it wasn't OCD. He genuinely believed that all his rituals were protecting him and us from certain death. He was utterly convinced that, if he stopped, we died. It was that simple.

He was so scared of stopping and I'm sure that's why he didn't respond to the initial treatment programme. He didn't want OCD to go away; he believed it was helping him keep us all alive.

Being referred to a specialist centre or seeking a more specialist opinion

I was determined that we couldn't just leave him like this; he had no life whatsoever. Fortunately for us, our local CAMHS team were just as determined and decided to seek advice from the Michael Rutter Centre in the Maudsley Hospital in London.

The Michael Rutter Centre has a national specialist centre for young people with OCD and there are a few around the country. The idea to have specialist centres came about in April 2007 to make sure that the most severe cases of refactory OCD are treated by the country's leading experts in the field. It's a great thing and every year they help hundreds of children who haven't responded to treatment locally. In case you were wondering, 'refactory' means 'doesn't respond to normal treatment'.

If you are referred to one of these centres, it's worth bearing in mind that, for most of us, it will involve travelling there and back, unless you're lucky enough to live in the area, of course. The centres are:

- The Maudsley Hospital, London
- Springfield University, London
- Royal Hospital Beckenham, Kent
- Queen Elizabeth II Hospital, Hertfordshire
- The Priory, London
- Sheffield Health and Social Care, Sheffield.

The clinic at the Maudsley is the most well known; they've even been on the telly! *Help Me Help My Child* is an excellent series on Channel 4 filmed in the Maudsley, as was *Growing Children: OCD* on the BBC, see if you can find them – they're well worth a watch.

When your local CAMHS service refers you to a specialist centre, the normal thing is for the family to be invited to the specialist centre for an assessment. Before you get there, though, you get about a phone book's worth of forms to fill in and get back to them. It was a good thing, though, because it meant that they had a pretty good idea of what was going on before we walked in the door. Again, I'm a great believer in writing everything down, and this was writing it down on a grand scale! The children get their own forms to fill in; my son would only fill two of them in, but it wasn't a problem – I just sent in what he'd done and it was still helpful to them. It takes about half a day and is pretty full on.

We arrived without a minute to spare at the Maudsley after an absolutely hellish three-hour journey (rush-hour traffic in central London + an OCD child who is terrified of being out of the house/travelling in a car + a Sat Nav that kept losing signal at crucial moments = stress to the power of five), not knowing what to expect.

So, we got in and sat down to wait to be called through. Our son was having a meltdown, refusing to go in, refusing to speak, and was generally very, very anxious, which was to be expected; it was a big deal. He didn't want to get better at that point, and felt that we were putting him and the rest of his family at risk of death by stopping him doing his rituals. He really felt that he had been chosen (by whom, he couldn't say) to protect us and, although he didn't like it, he had no choice. It was us that didn't understand.

Then the wonderful Dr Heyman came out and invited us to go through. Our son refused. I looked at Dr Heyman, she looked at me, I looked at my partner, we didn't know what to do. The thing is, it's quite embarrassing. No parent wants their child to be rude or difficult in public, it's mortifying. Even when you know there's a good reason for it, you can't help feeling like a failure because you can't get your child to express good manners. We felt as if Dr Heyman would see us as bad parents, having allowed our son to be totally out of our control and clearly rude.

And, we were tired. Not just not-had-enough sleep tired, we were emotionally tired. We'd been fighting our son for every inch for a couple of years by that point and I confess I just wanted to shout at him, 'Will you just help us, just this once, can't you just be easy for a change?'

Then, I felt guilty for feeling like that because, of course, he can't help it. But, I'm only human. I didn't shout at him, I did what a lot of parents will do in that situation...

I plastered a big smile on my face, laughed, effected a jolly, upper-class voice and said loudly, 'Come on, up you get, time to go,' sweeping my arm back and forth as if I could waft him off his chair. Nerves and embarrassment had turned me into my headmistress. All I needed was a pleated woollen skirt, a knitted cardie and sensible walking shoes.

He didn't budge. Thank God for the good doctor. She spoke to him for just a few minutes and up he got, and off he went. I didn't know whether to feel relieved or offended that she'd only known him for ten minutes and could already get him to do things I couldn't.

Off they marched, down the corridor, my partner and I trailing behind like the extra baggage we felt we were, and into a room filled with people. There was even a one-way mirror at one end of the room, which I tried not to be fascinated by and resisted the urge to make faces into. Nerves make me a bit weird, you see, and I was pretty sure that I needed to appear as stable as possible for this meeting. No need to order a psych evaluation for the mother today, people, thank you very much.

We were introduced to everyone. There were psychologists and psychiatrists and others that I was never sure what they did, but they all seemed very nice and took great care to make us all feel as comfortable as possible. We talked in that room for about half an hour and then we were asked to go into a separate room to talk with half of the team, leaving our son with the rest. Preparing for an outburst of mammoth proportions I plastered my big smile back on my face and looked at our son, expecting him to be shaking his head and ready to flee.

He was smiling. The little toad was actually smiling, and agreeing that that was fine. The child who had refused to be near strangers for two years, shrugged and said, 'OK.'

Don't get me wrong, I was very happy that he was feeling well enough to do that. It was great that he was actually being easy, that's what I wanted. But, for goodness sake, why wouldn't he do that for me? Was it me? Did I in some way contribute to his problem? Was that second GP right, and this was all attention seeking because I wasn't showing him enough love?

Having spoken to the team about this in the months since, I've realised that no, it's not me. I don't contribute to the problem. He was just trying to please, and too shy really to make a fuss. When it's just me, he does not have such issues.

I have also now convinced myself that the people at the Maudsley know Jedi mind tricks. It gets me through the day.

In the other room, my partner and I were asked a lot of questions about our son's early development, how he played as a toddler, when he started talking etc. As we were telling them about these things, we realised that his problem had started as early as two years old, we just didn't recognise it. My partner reminded me about the washing machine obsession (as I have already mentioned in Chapter 1) and I almost slapped my forehead. Oh God, the washing machine!

How could we not have realised that something was up? He was our first child, we didn't know, and kids get crazes, don't they? Yes, they do, and not all go on to develop full-blown OCD, of course. We just couldn't believe how far back his symptoms had started.

While we were in there, the rest of the team were assessing our son's level of OCD. To do this a test called the CY-BOCS (more abbreviations: this one stands for Children's Yale-Brown Obsessive Compulsive Scale) is used and you end up with a score out of 40. The levels are:

0–7	Subclinical OCD
8–15	Mild OCD
16–23	Moderate OCD
24–31	Severe OCD
32–40	Extreme OCD

The test is really a tick box thing, and takes into account how many rituals are done, how often, how much anxiety is experienced if they don't do a ritual, how it interferes in their life, how much they try to resist their rituals and how much control they have over their rituals. The same things are taken into account with the obsessions they experience. It's a measure of how much impact OCD is having on your child's life.

Our son's score was 37. Not good.

The Maudsley have different streams within their service. They often see people who have had treatment locally, but the young person hasn't responded to treatment. If a young person has had a course of CBT and a course of medication (SSRI's) and still has OCD in the severe range, they can access the service without having to have the funding from the PCT. The reason for this is they have a stream of funding from the National Specialised Commissioning Team (NSCT); previously known as the NCG. The Department of Health fund the service so young people who meet the criteria can get the Maudsley's help without any extra funding from their local PCT. It's so everyone can have a fair and equal access to specialised treatment if and when they need it. Often, children can overcome OCD with CBT given by their local services, so this funding is just for those cases that don't.

The reason this test is so important is that the Maudsley can only take patients outside of their Primary Care Trust (PCT) if they fall in the 'extreme' category, and Steps 1–5 of the NICE guidelines have been followed, and haven't worked. This is why I said it is important in the long run to follow the NICE guidelines because if you don't, there is a chance it could impact on accessing more help if you need it. So, play ball, it's worth it.

There are two ways that treatment at a specialist centre can be funded:

• your local PCT pays
• the NCG pays.

OK, pause for an abbreviation update. PCT stands for Primary Care Trust: the governing body of your local NHS services. NCG stands for National Commissioning Group: a group commissioned by the Department of Health that have a pot of cash used to fund treatment for the worst cases, so that they don't have to waste treatment time applying to the PCT for funding.

The best way to get funding is through the NSCT. That makes it quicker and more straightforward as getting funding through your PCT is a complicated business and they don't like parting with their cash. To get funding from the NSCT, you have to be able to prove:

- OCD is above 30 on the CY-BOCS scale
- had a course of CBT including ERP
- had a course of medication for OCD to the maximum dose.

For us, unfortunately, this is where things got a little sticky. Although we clearly qualified on the CY-BOCS score, and we knew we had followed the guidelines, it emerged that the therapist who had been working with our son for over a year had no formal qualifications in ERP therapy. So, there was doubt that the NICE guidelines had been followed and that a combination of CBT and ERP had been given.

It took a couple of weeks for this news to be delivered to us. We were told that we had to apply to our local PCT for funding and I knew that this was going to be a fight. It felt very unfair, we had enough on our plates, and now I had to write justifications and lobby a PCT panel to persuade them that our son needed the help of a Centre of Excellence. There was no guarantee that this was going to be successful and, in fact, the likelihood was that they would say that we had to start at the beginning again, and work with another therapist who had the formal qualifications required.

I felt angry for a few reasons: (i) Why was my son not being looked after by someone with the right qualifications? (ii) Why was my son being penalised because our local PCT didn't supply those therapists? (iii) Was my son as bad as he was because he hadn't received the correct therapy?

I have to say, in our local therapist's defence, I knew that he had been doing ERP in the sessions. By that time I'd read enough to know what it was and I also knew that I'd been doing it with my son at home all the time. We just didn't tick the box that read 'ERP by a qualified ERP therapist'.

Our local CAMHS team were good, though; they jumped in and started sending letters to the Maudsley outlining the detail of the sessions our son had had. (Why don't the NHS use emails in this day and age? I can't understand why we have to wait days for letters – it makes no sense to me.) They fought to have it recognised that the local therapist, whilst, no, he had not done a specialist ERP training course, was a hugely experienced therapist who had covered ERP as part of his general training. They also argued that I had been doing ERP at home, which I had, and that just going to a therapy session every other week was ERP as our son was terrified of leaving the house, driving in a car and being with other people.

Finally, after quite a bit of to-ing and fro-ing, the Maudsley were able to prove that NICE guidelines had been followed and our son did, in fact, qualify for NSCT funding.

Nothing's ever simple, but we got there in the end. This process took about four months, though, and our son was getting worse every day. By this point he was hardly eating and most of his daily calories came from Skittles.

So, do yourself a favour, make sure the NICE guidelines are followed. Ask for details of your therapist's training and experience, and don't be afraid to say if you feel that they don't have everything the guidelines say they should. It'll save you a lot of time later if you need more help.

For those of you whose treatment is funded by your insurance, I have read that similar funding rules can apply; it really depends on how your insurance covers mental health conditions. I've heard that some insurance companies will allow the therapist to dictate the course of treatment and they will provide funding according to need, but I've also heard stories where insurance companies refuse to cover certain treatments unless other, sometimes less expensive, treatments have been tried first. It's really worth calling your insurance company to find out exactly how funding is released and approved to ensure that you are doing everything according to their guidelines, and so ensure that your child receives the care they need when they need it.

If you need help or advice I've found that OCD organisations are extremely helpful; they have up-to-date information and usually provide advocacy with funding and education should you need it. You can find your country's group online, there is also an OCD resources and websites scetion at the end of the book.

TIPS

✶ Understand that sometimes a child is too afraid to fight OCD. Be patient.

✶ Don't take it personally if your child will do things for therapists they won't do for you – it means you've taught them good manners!

✶ Make sure your therapist is providing both CBT and ERP therapy.

✶ Ask for your child to be measured on the CY-BOCS scale.

✶ Above all, I'll say it again…it is not your fault!

Being admitted to a mental health facility

Those words make me shudder. They struck fear in me from the very first time I heard them, and they still do. My child? In a mental health facility? No way. That doesn't happen to people like us! We don't belong there!

Sometimes, children do need to be admitted if their OCD is compromising their physical health, their safety or the safety of those around them, or if their OCD needs intense therapy to crack it. In our son's case, it was his physical health that made admission necessary. He was underweight and exhausted. His eating problems were getting worse and he was malnourished. I tried to feed him, I tried everything, I really did, but he wouldn't eat it.

It took me a long time to accept that it had to happen. If I'm honest, I don't think I ever completely did. I hated the idea so much, I instinctively rejected it the second anyone mentioned it. Like an ostrich with my head in the sand... it just wasn't happening. I'm not stupid – I knew he was underweight, I knew he was exhausted. I knew that couldn't carry on. I knew all of that. I just couldn't accept that I couldn't fix it. That I couldn't make him better, or stop him getting worse, at least.

We had a few months between the prospect of admission being raised and then it being planned. I was so sure it wouldn't come to that. But it did.

Our son took the news a lot better than I thought he would, actually. He didn't want to go, and at times, he insisted he wasn't going and his anxiety levels were very high, but he knew he needed to. By this point, he wanted to get better, and he knew he needed more help than I could give him to achieve that.

What a sentence for a mother to hear: 'You can't give him what he needs.' I knew it was true, and everybody was very quick and took great care to explain that it wasn't that I wasn't capable or not doing a good job, it was just that his OCD had a real grip on him and he needed to be somewhere that was out of his comfort zone and doing ERP 24 hours per day. With staff that he wouldn't refuse to cooperate with.

So logical, of course, it made absolute sense. In my heart of hearts I knew that getting him out of this house would be the best thing for him. I knew he was far too dependent on me, and that the house didn't challenge his OCD because it was just as he wanted it. Yes, getting away, facing OCD head on, tackling it, fighting, it would be brutal but it was the right thing.

My head said that. My heart was screaming that a mother never walks away when her child is in distress.

Just as I said before, a child with OCD will feel all the fear and anxiety as if their life really is in danger, and somehow, as a parent, you have to make them confront that, without the comfort that it is instinctive to give them. Admitting him into a facility, walking away when he screamed and begged me not to? Leaving him with strangers who didn't know him when he was terrified? Trusting strangers to know how to help him? It was against every single maternal instinct I had. But, I had to do it, for him. I was worried that they didn't know him as well as I do, that they wouldn't know how to distract him as easily. I hated the idea that he would feel unable to tell them difficult things and might struggle with something in silence.

OCD rips your heart out, doesn't it? I can honestly say that the day he was admitted was an all-time low. It was dreadful – I felt completely desolate; our son felt completely terrified. That first week, in fact, was dreadful.

I found myself feeling jealous of the nursing staff. I felt quite threatened by them actually. It got worse as he began to settle in and respond to treatment. I was thrilled he was improving, but I felt so jealous that they could do something for him that I couldn't. It's a reflection of my own feelings of guilt and sense of failure, I suppose; certainly the staff there didn't ever do or say anything to make me feel that way. It was just me.

Suddenly, our son was chatting to other people, happy to be in their company, not worried if I didn't come during the afternoon visiting hours. This was great news, and I was absolutely delighted for him. For me...I was a little bit crushed. It had been him and me, in it together, for so long, I found the adjustment hard to make. His independence was crucial to me, and yet, I missed him.

I found myself feeling left out. I didn't feel part of the solution anymore, as if it had been decided that I couldn't help and so, responsibility was taken out of my hands. I got the impression that they felt he and I were too close, and that I was part of the problem. The more I tried to remain involved, the stronger I felt this. I don't really know if they did think that, or if it was just me being silly but I must say, it felt very real.

There were weekly meetings, where I was given his progress report and an opportunity to ask questions or give feedback...once a week. This is my child, he may not have been a baby, but he was my child and I was having to endure days of not knowing how much he had eaten, how his therapy was going, if his rituals were getting better. I knew that he was still doing a lot of rituals when he was alone in his room, and I did tell them this. I also told them that he was doing this secretly to allow him to be seen to be doing less, and so bring discharge closer. He wasn't being entirely honest, driven by a need to be discharged, but he had made improvements and, most importantly, was learning how resilient he can be. If he could do that, surely he could do anything.

For me, though, I just missed him. The staff would smile at me and say, 'You must be enjoying the rest?' in a sunny tone. I wanted to shout, 'I can't sleep while I know he's here anxious! What kind of mother do you think I am?' but I didn't. I didn't want them to think I was an overbearing mother, so I agreed that it was a treat. I guess a lot of parents experience similar feelings when children fly the nest, don't they? There he was, not needing me as much. It's what I wanted, but, yes, it hurt and it took some getting used to.

He was discharged from the facility after eight weeks and he had improved. He was eating a bit better, sleeping better and sleeping on his bed even! That was a real thrill, seeing him on his bed, rather than on a mattress on the floor. If you recall, OCD made him believe that something terrible would happen if he touched his bed, so it was one in the eye for OCD!

Our experience of admission was emotionally difficult, as you'd expect, but worth it. So very worth it. He didn't come out of there cured, not by a long way, but, he came out with the major concerns improved, and with more self-confidence. He had done something he didn't think he could do, and he felt good about himself. That's proved more helpful in the continued fight against OCD than anything – he is learning that he can do this, he deserves a better life, and that he is stronger than he thought he was. Even if that was the only change, it would have been worth it.

So, don't be too afraid if your child needs to be admitted. Yes, it will be tough on you, yes, you will be upset and maybe even a bit irrational. But it's worth it.

TIPS

★ Have confidence! In yourself, and in your child. The more your child believes in their own strength and resilience – the easier it will be for them to fight OCD.

★ The only way to learn about resilience is to prove it! Don't be scared to put your child in a challenging environment; it can often be the best thing for them.

★ If your child is in a challenging environment, try not to let them leave until the anxiety has died down, without rituals! This is how they will learn about their own inner strength, rather than rely on rituals.

★ If your child is admitted – you'll get through it. You'll find a way and you will get through it. Eyes on the prize.

★ Sometimes it's hard when your child comes to rely on someone else. Accept the normality of this, and the normality of your own feelings. All parents feel this at some point.

CHAPTER 5

School

Educating the Educators

Is our son well enough for school? That was a question I asked myself every day from the beginning of Year 6, when he was ten. He wasn't sleeping well. He was very anxious about going to school. He was scared of the other children, the germs, the numbers, the open windows. He wasn't eating well.

If our youngest son had a bad night, and was really tired the next day, I'd keep him off school and let him catch up on his sleep. But, with my eldest, I was pushing him and cajoling him every morning that he was going to go, saying he would be fine, there was no reason not to go. It didn't feel fair, and I know our eldest felt very strongly that it wasn't fair.

When our son got his diagnosis, I went in and spoke to his headteacher. She seemed quite unfazed by it, telling me that she had experience with OCD and understood the challenges, so she was sure they could accommodate, and work with, our son. Phew, I thought, that's all right then.

But it wasn't all right.

Year 6 SATs loomed large. (These are exams taken by students in the UK at around 11 years old, prior to moving to their next school. These exams are used to assess the performance of both student and school, so schools have a lot riding on them.) Our son's psychiatrist felt that our son shouldn't be pushed to do them as his anxiety level was already very high, and the test wasn't for his personal benefit, it was for the school. So, I went in again and spoke to his headteacher. She was keen for our son to take the SATs, and as our son wanted to take them (he didn't want to be different and was worried about how to explain that to other students), I agreed provided we could come up with a plan that would give him the best chance of success, taking into account his individual needs.

The headteacher told me that he would write his tests in a separate room, with a teacher with him, and they would be allowed to take breaks. OK, I thought, we'll see what happens.

SATs cover English and maths. Our son is really good at English, he loves to read and write stories, so I wasn't too worried about that except for his problem with numbers. He is afraid of odd numbers, you see, to the point that he won't answer questions 1, 3, 5, 7, 9 etc etc. even on his English test. I knew this would impact his result and as for a maths test, well, I just couldn't see how it would work.

My main worry wasn't about the school, or even his anxiety while he was writing the actual test, I knew enough about anxiety to know it'd pass but what worried me was how he'd feel about himself if he got a poor result. His condition had led to him having pretty low self-esteem as it was, and getting rubbish marks on a test that he'd tried so hard for, well, I was concerned about how that would affect him.

I was very proud of him for doing it, though. He always says he's a coward because he's scared of so many things, but all I can see is massive bravery when he does something even though he's terrified. As I say to him often, 'You fight monsters, you're the bravest boy in the world.'

As it turned out, he did very well in his English SAT and not so well on his maths (no surprises there, then). Thank God he got a good English mark, because that helped soften the maths blow and he was able to see that his low mark was because of his difficulties, not a lack of intelligence.

After SATs, our son only had a matter of weeks to get through to the end of the school year, and the end of his time at that school. I must say that our son's difficulties were over-indulged during that period of time, and I felt that this was because he was soon going to be another school's problem. Our son missed quite a lot of school in those months, and when he was there he mostly sat in the support teacher's office, and made them all cups of tea. A proper education? I think not. But he couldn't do much more than that at the time – it was amazing he was even there.

So, that's the thing about schools. Three things can happen: they may be concerned about the impact on the school and their budgets, they may just not care or, they may be brilliant and give you some much-needed support, help you fight your child's OCD and keep them in school.

What you know, and how you approach them, can make a huge difference, though, so read up about your local council's provisions for children who have mental health problems.

It may be helpful to have your child assessed for a Statement of Special Educational Needs, soon to be renamed as an Education, Health and Social Care Plan. (We were advised by our local psychiatrist to do so but we didn't do it.) This is a document that describes in detail what your child's needs are, what support they should receive and what help must be provided to them. A Statement of Special Educational Needs is a legal document and schools have to provide the support that it advises. So, basically, if your child needs support because they have a fear of germs, so going to the toilet is difficult at school and prevents them attending regularly, the Statement of Special Educational Needs will outline what steps need to be put in place to help.

To get one, you should inform the school that you would like a Statutory Assessment to be carried out on your child. The local education authority should then assess your child by observing them at home and at school for a period of time, so that they can work out what support is needed. Once this is done, and a statement is issued for your child, the school must comply. Even if they need to hire someone to be with your child all day, like a Learning Support Assistant to work directly with your child, it has to be done. It's your security that, no matter what school they go to, their needs will be met, and they will get an education.

In the United States, the education of children with special educational needs is covered by the Individuals with Disabilities Education Act (IDEA), which is a federal law that governs how states make provisions for children with disabilities from age 3 to 18 or 21. The Act requires that all public schools create an Individualized Education Program (IEP) for each eligible student, which will specify what services must be provided to support the child through their education. There has been some bad press about implementing the actual IEPs in school, with some parents finding some schools to be quite uncooperative. There appear to be some problems with funding, as schools are expected to fund a large percentage of the costs themselves with only a small grant from Congress. So, as with most things, it's not perfect. But, your child does have rights. Wherever you are in the world, your child has the right to an education. Your child has the right to expect support with a disability and reasonable provisions to be made to help them access education. It may be with OCD that your child would benefit from having their own helper, to help them manage rituals in class, or get around the school more easily; it will all depend on your child's symptoms and how they uniquely affect your child in school.

All that said, of course, we should never give in to OCD's demands. The more we make changes to accommodate OCD, the more it wants. But, when you're faced with a choice of your child not attending school because they can't use the toilet and is very anxious about that, or attending school with support... I think you have to prioritise education in the short term. That's not to say that you shouldn't be working towards your child being able to use the toilet (or whatever the fear is) but, it should be addressed when you reach that fear in your therapy sessions. So, it should be temporary, and should only ever be viewed as that. Don't let OCD get too comfy, or, just like the toddler in the previous chapter, it'll scream and scream for more, because you've shown it that you will give in.

So, why didn't you do that? I hear you ask. Well, because he became so ill, and had so many problems, that I knew no amount of support in school would help him attend.

The day he started senior school...all hell broke loose. I knew that the change was going to be challenging. Our son doesn't respond well to change, as is the case with most OCD sufferers, and the change was going to be quite a big one. He'd been at the same primary school his whole school life and it was a really small school, where he was very familiar with the staff and they knew him well. So, it was a safe place. Well, not quite safe, he still battled his anxiety to go during his last year there but it was certainly less overwhelming for him. So, he was going to have to go from a small school where he'd been for seven years with about 150 pupils total, to a huge school with more than 1800 pupils, moving classrooms and having different teachers for each lesson.

This would require some planning. I asked for a meeting with the SENCO at his new senior school in the June before he was due to start, and she came to his primary school to talk about integrating him into the new environment.

Abbreviation alert: SENCO stands for Special Educational Needs Coordinator. All schools in the UK have at least one for a small school and quite a few for a larger school. This is someone to make friends with; a good relationship with your SENCO will make a big difference to your child's education. Outside of the UK, this role is usually performed by a school counsellor, whose job it is to provide support for any learning or health concerns.

Aside from all his OCD fears, our son had suffered severe bullying and this also had a massive impact on his mental well-being. Bullying can be a common problem for children with OCD, as their rituals can draw attention and come across as odd. It makes them different, and when you're a kid, different isn't good.

Beating the bullies on the outside while fighting the bully in your head

OK, so, in your child's head lives a bully. It puts horrible thoughts in their heads, horrible images, and makes them do things they don't really want to do because they are scared of the threats their bully makes. That's how OCD operates. Then, to make matters worse, not only do they carry that bully around all the time, very often there are other bullies in the 'real world' that think it's hilarious that your child taps, or counts or is scared of something.

Our son became, in his words, 'the school freak'. With the exception of one or two children, every child in that school had something to say. He never knew when it was coming, or who it was going to come from. There were ring leaders, of course, and they made his life hell. It got so bad that even children from other schools who didn't know our son would chant and follow him if he was at the park. Or worse.

He has been pushed to the ground while they forced pictures of clowns in his face (he is very scared of clowns), him lying there and just screaming and screaming because, not only was there a picture of a clown, there was a crowd of people touching him and pulling at him, with all the germs and fears that come along with that. Him becoming hysterical was fuel to the fire, the funniest thing ever, apparently, because his scream was high-pitched, like a girl's they said. So, they would take every chance they could to make him scream like that. Given his fear of germs, it wasn't hard for them; mostly all they had to do was walk near him and push him gently. They thought he was screaming because even a gentle push hurt him or he was so threatened by them that even close proximity was enough to terrify him. They didn't know it wasn't them, it was their germs.

Then it was just small things, but no less awful. Because of his fearfulness and screaming, everyone told him he was a girl, and his best friend was a girl. So, when asked to line up in rows of boys and girls, our son had to suffer the taunts of being in the wrong row, whispered quietly so the teacher couldn't hear. Kids can be so cruel.

Not that the teachers always helped. One teacher, upon dismissing the class at the end of a Friday, told the class to 'have a nice weekend, don't forget your art homework' and then added, looking straight at my son, 'Perhaps you'll draw me a clown, what do you think?' which was followed by loud laughing from the rest of the class, and he joined in. It was devastatingly embarrassing for my son, a real abuse of trust, I felt. When confronted, the teacher apologised and claimed he hadn't known the extent of my son's problems, and maybe that's true but it was insensitive at best, from a person supposed to be in a position of authority, a role model for the other children.

The SENCO at that school was marvellous though. She got us through with her constant concern and genuine caring for our son and his situation. There should be more like her; she is a credit to the school and we will be forever in her debt. She was always there for us, and watched over our son like he was one of her own. If it weren't for her, he wouldn't have attended school in Year 6 as regularly as he did. She made it possible.

I was up at the school so often, trying to keep him in school, trying to get the school to help him, trying to stop other kids targeting him the way they did. To be fair to the headteacher, she did react to serious complaints, and some children were disciplined as a result. It broke my heart how my son reacted to this, though, and still makes me have a little weep when I think of it.

There was a particular boy who delighted in making my son's life as difficult as possible. He led a campaign of mockery and abuse that terrified my son, that made him cower into walls if he walked near him. I hated seeing my son do that. I've always despised bullies, and have stood up to them whenever I have come across them in my life. It was hard to see him so meek, so submissive. I wanted him to stand up to that boy, no matter what that brought. I'd rather get a punch in the face than see them beat me. My frustration didn't help my son, though, it just made him feel even more inadequate, comparing himself to me, so I had to stop coaching him on what to do, what to say. He was just too scared, and he wasn't me.

Anyway, after a particularly bad incident with this boy in school, I complained and this boy's parents were called in. This happened during the school day and, when the meeting was over, the boy was sent back to class. He was clearly upset, still crying, with puffy red eyes and a runny nose. Now, my reaction to that was, 'Good, glad someone's finally got through to him, maybe now he'll realise how unacceptable his behaviour is and he'll stop.' The other children, previously so admiring of him, all avoided him, not making eye contact and feeling uncomfortable to see this former hero of theirs crying, so he sat alone in the corner, looking very sorry for himself. One child in that class felt for him. One child in that class had the courage to go over to him and ask if he was OK. One child wanted to help.

Our son.

Our son, who had been terrorised by this boy for months, who knew this boy delighted in making him feel awful, was the only one to approach him and ask if he was OK.

That's a common thing with kids with OCD. They're very sensitive and my son has an awful lot of empathy for people around him. He feels sorry for everybody and would help anyone. My feelings were torn. On the one hand, I was so proud of him, he was the better person and is such a lovely boy. On the other hand, I wanted him to feel a bit less concerned for others, and a bit more concerned about himself, to see that what was happening to him was unacceptable, that he didn't deserve it and the children doing it should be disciplined for it. But, he'll never do that, he takes no pleasure in other people's distress, even though so many seem to take pleasure in his.

Look out for signs of bullying; it's common and makes life even harder. Try to keep communication open with your child so they feel able to talk to you if something bad is happening to them and, if it is, make it known to the school. Don't leave it – it's not acceptable. They must, and will, act.

Understanding of mental illness is patchy in education. If you do decide to talk to your child's school about their OCD, it's a good idea to lend them some books on the subject as they may not be fully aware of how this can affect a child in the context of education. You also need their support in watching out for signs of bullying or other problems with children in class. If your child is comfortable with it, it helps if the school teach children about OCD. It promotes understanding, and sends the message that any kind of bullying would not be tolerated. There is a great book available that was written to help schools do this called *Can I Tell You About OCD?* (Jessica Kingsley Publishers, 2013) it's written by Dr Amita Jassi, Clinical Psychologist at the National OCD Service for Young People at the Maudsley Hospital (and also my son's totally amazing therapist!). I would advise you to get a copy and present the school with it, after you've read it yourself and let other family members read it. It's a brilliant book, aimed at young people who know someone with OCD. It's also great for the sufferer…an all-round gem and well worth the price.

Back to senior school

I went off on one about bullying there, didn't I? Where was I? Oh yes, I was having a meeting with our son's SENCO from senior school.

So, we had a meeting and I told her about our son's condition and my concerns about how the transition could affect him and came up with a plan of two or three extra visits to the school for our son and me, to get him more used to the school environment. We'd be able to meet the Heads of House and Year and talk them through all my son's difficulties, which I thought seemed very sensible.

We had the two meetings. The first one was to meet his Head of House and the Head of Year and then I asked if they could appoint two Year 11 mentors, selected by the staff, kids who they felt had the compassion and the maturity to be able to understand what my son was going through, and be able to help when needed. We met them, along with the Heads of House and Year and the Head of Pastoral Care, in the second meeting.

This often helps, having slightly older kids involved. They take the responsibility very seriously and your child often feels more able to talk to another pupil than a teacher if they are concerned about something, or are having difficulties. Most schools are happy to do it.

In the second meeting, I took an OCD pack for each of the people attending. In it I included basic information on what OCD is, the list that you saw in Chapter 1, a suggested reading guide and a link to OCD Action, who have an online initiative called OCD At School, full of useful resources for teachers as well as forums to ask questions and get advice from other teachers who have worked with young people with OCD (see the OCD Resources and Websites section at the end of this book). I talked them through all of my son's rituals, the ways they might impact on his education, like being late for class if he gets 'stuck' on the stairs, doing rituals in class, anxiety about eating at lunchtime, being scared of numbers and I tried to explain it all as honestly and openly as I could. As I read it all out, I felt sick, though. It made it all very real. He was really bad. It was a proper cold water in the face moment.

I tried to prepare them. They seemed very sincere in their desire to make this a successful transition, and they did do their best. The problem was, it's a big school, with a lot of pupils and staff. And nothing prepared me for what was to come.

The first day came and I dropped him off in his crisp new uniform and his new haircut. He was actually feeling quite positive. That whole day I sat at home and fretted about how he was doing and when it was time to pick him up at the end of the school day, I sat outside in my car, heart pounding, desperately begging to see a smile on his face as he walked out of the gate. I knew I had sent him into a situation that he might find very hard and he was my baby. God, I wanted nothing more than to wrap him up and keep him safe.

Then I saw him and, he was smiling! The relief that flooded through me – if I hadn't been sitting down, I swear my knees would have gone out from under me. He jumped into the car, full of the day he'd had and I sat with tears in my eyes as I watched my timid little boy laugh and proudly show me his very complicated timetable. Normal. He looked like a normal, happy boy. That, my friends, was an absolutely priceless moment. I rewind to that moment in my mind often; it helps me see the boy underneath the OCD, a glimpse of the real boy, carefree, not scared, not worried, just...free.

Day 2 dawned and I dropped him off again. He was a bit quiet, but he hadn't slept well, as usual, so I put it down to that. He didn't refuse to go and I was feeling quite positive. When the time came to pick him up, and I hadn't received a call from the school saying something was wrong, I was light of heart and looking forward to hearing his news.

I knew something was wrong as soon as I caught sight of him. Head down, shuffling, arms drawn in, shoulders hunched, wincing in the middle of the throng of pupils flooding through the gate. He struck an odd figure, my lovely boy, scuttling and shuffling, like all the other children were on fast forward and he alone was in real time. I wanted to jump out of the car and scoop him up but I didn't, that would have been worse for him, so I waited for him to make his way to me. When he got into the car, he sat and rocked back and forth in the seat, hyperventilating, unable to tell me what was wrong. He wouldn't let me touch him to offer any comfort so we drove home, him rocking and making the sign of the cross, me feeling sick and helpless.

When he managed to calm down enough to tell me what had happened, it emerged that he had got stuck running up and down the stairs that he had to climb between classes and a group of boys had noticed him and started laughing and calling others. He was 'stuck' going up and down the stairs for about 20 minutes until finally, when he was exhausted, OCD let him try to find his class. He knew where the class was but, to get there, he had to go past the woodwork class, a room with saws and other blades inside. He couldn't walk past it. So he fled to the office to find the Pastoral Care Officer, who wasn't around, and he just sat there waiting until the end of the day.

I called the school and spoke to his Head of House, who was my point of contact and she was upset to hear his experience and vowed to try and find a member of staff to accompany him between classes the next day.

But, that didn't happen. It couldn't happen. I don't blame them – they didn't have the staff to do that.

On the third day, they called me to bring my son home. He had been in his Tech class and his group were doing sewing that term. Needles everywhere, my son had a massive urge to stick a needle in his eye. Bravely, he went to the teacher and told her, because that's what he had been told to do. They were all supposed to have been told about his condition and what could happen.

The Tech teacher had not been told. In my son's words she 'looked at him like he was a serial killer' and sent him to the office, where he fell apart and begged them to call me. So, they did.

On Day 4, I went in with him and spoke again to his Head of House, asking why the Tech teacher hadn't been updated. She didn't know and, again, apologised. I left our son with her but they called me back later that day after he had got 'stuck' on the stairs again and couldn't get off. The worst thing was how humiliated he felt. All those people seeing him that way, seeing him in that state was awful for him, he hated himself. I can imagine how embarrassing that must have been, can't you? At an age when all you want is to fit in, if you don't it's a terrible thing.

Day 5 came and he didn't go in. He'd not slept at all and was having a full-blown panic attack at 7:30am so there was no way I could get him there. I called the school and the SENCO called me back at about lunchtime and asked if she could come out and see me. She came on the Monday. My son wasn't at school again following a dreadful weekend of no sleep (literally) and very little food. The SENCO informed me that it was felt by the school that they were not equipped to cope with my son's needs and they were, therefore, referring him to our local education authority's provision for the education of children unable to access school: a one-to-one tutor who comes to your home.

And that was the end of school.

At the time, it was a dreadful blow. We'd tried so hard to keep him in school, to keep his life as normal as possible, to give this bright, intelligent boy an education. More failure.

OCD: 1 – Parents: nil

Then, we met Mr Alavi. He was to be my son's tutor and would come to our home for an hour every day. Mr A has been an absolute godsend. I can't praise the provision made for my son highly enough. He has been a source of support, he has helped with therapy, he has educated himself about my son's condition and is the most compassionate, dedicated teacher I have ever met.

He's been working with my son for about two years now, and is like one of the family. For me, he's often there when things are tough as my son regularly finds it difficult to come downstairs for lessons as Mr A teaches other kids and may, therefore, have an illness, or so my son thinks. So he's seen my son at his worst, and he's seen me try to deal with that. But, he's never lost patience, never made me feel as if it's a problem; he's always utterly focused on my son's needs and wanting to work with me to improve his condition. He's helped enormously with that. From introducing cooking classes (which aren't part of the home tutor curriculum) to persuading my son to eat more, to gradually introducing maths to help him deal with odd numbers, to constructing lessons around things that most interest my son so that he will get more enjoyment from them, and access them more easily.

Mr A has been instrumental in maintaining a constant in my son's life and we'll never be able to repay him for that. He remains part of our son's trusted inner circle, his 'go-to guy' when things get tricky and to be able to build that kind of bond with a child like our son is a gift. Everyone should have a Mr A in their life. We were very, very lucky.

OCD: 1 – Parents: 1

Outside of the UK, the education provisions vary widely. Speak to your child's local school for adivce, they are best placed to know what help may be out there, or point you in the right direction to find out for yourself. Also, your OCD groups will have information for you, I've included the main groups later on in the book, they're invaluable. If that fails, speak to your therapist, speak to your local governing bodies, speak to anyone, everyone! Don't stop pushing!

Our area also has a bespoke unit called the EV Unit, for Emotionally Vulnerable children. This was our next goal.

The difference the right school can make

After being discharged from the mental health facility, our son was offered a place at the EV Unit and he was keen to go. He's been attending for a few months now and the road hasn't been smooth, to say the least. The effect on his actual

OCD has been difficult; there are so many triggers he has to contend with: the germs he feels the other students and the staff may be harbouring, saying something offensive, hurting someone, sharp objects...you name it, he's facing it there. But, he's facing it. He has deteriorated since leaving hospital, has some new rituals and his anxiety is worse than ever, if I'm honest but that's because he's still doing rituals.

The effect on his confidence has been dramatic. He is well liked by everyone there, has made friends, and is really beginning to come out of his shell. In the fight against OCD, this confidence, this belief in his own strength, the support of friends, these are the things that will give him the courage to fight, these are his weapons. He may not be able to use them very effectively at the moment, but he'll learn. In time, I have every confidence that he will feel strong enough to stop the rituals. In a gradual way, with support, of course, but I believe the confidence he is gaining in himself is making the boy inside slowly grow bigger than OCD – it's just a matter of time.

I can't advise you strongly enough to keep your child in school if at all possible. It is crucial to their recovery to have some confidence. If the school your child attends isn't helping with that, if you can, find another school, find somewhere that will provide a nurturing but challenging environment that you can work with. It doesn't matter if your child attends school irregularly. It doesn't matter if they don't attend all their classes, or if they aren't able to concentrate when they make it into class. The more your child goes to school and keeps hold of that normality, the stronger they will become and the weaker OCD will become. It won't make it go away, but it will help to keep your child's confidence level up, and that is crucial in the fight.

Of course, all of this is very easy to say. Please don't think I'm over-simplifying it. I know what it's like when your child is panicking and refusing to go to school. Sometimes you just can't get them there. It may not even be safe to transport them in the car if they're panicking, so please don't get the idea that I think it's easy. It's not. The thing I found most useful is to drill down to exactly what about school is scary for our son. He'll say to me, 'I'm just scared to go to school' and at his age, the way their minds work, that's the truth. But, if I talk to him about it and ask some key questions, I am able to find out exactly what the fear is. It may be the germs he's worried other students are carrying or it may be he's worrying about swearing. Finding out what the specific fear is helps because then you can do something about it. OCD likes to generalise, so our weapon needs to be specifics. He's not afraid of school, he's afraid of germs. We can help that fear with ERP. Breaking it down means that you can attack the fears at their root, rather than a wide, scattergun approach that misses the target.

We are so lucky to have the EV Unit. The staff there have chosen to work with children who display a range of different behaviours, largely due to anxiety problems. They are patient, yet push our son, they are tolerant and understanding, yet impose discipline where required. They're incredible and they are making the difference for our son.

For me, getting him up in the morning and taking him to school is a real treat. Yes, he's anxious, yes, mornings are difficult and he often doesn't want to go, but he does go. It's still a thrill for me to hear about the students he's friends with and what they got up to that day, to wait for him at the school gates again. It feels more normal and I feel more positive about the future. It makes me so proud and so humbled by the strength and determination he's showing. He wants a future and OCD is trying to do its level best to make his future uncertain and isolated. Every time he goes to school, when OCD is telling him about the hundreds of dangers, is a victory and proof that he can do it.

We are extremely lucky to have this specialist unit local to us for our son to attend, and there are many that don't have this luxury, I know. If your child has no choice but to attend a regular mainstream school, then there are things that you and the teaching staff can do to make the experience easier. Regardless of how your child's OCD is manifesting itself, managing the anxiety is the key. Make sure all staff are aware of how to react if your child becomes anxious. This may be encouraging your child to wait the anxiety out, or distracting them from the anxiety, whatever you and your child's therapist have found to be the best solution. Also, provide a way for your child to alert their teacher to an OCD problem without having to announce it. For our son, it was very difficult to raise his hand in class and explain what was happening, so the staff gave him a card to rest on his desk. One side was green and the other red. If he was OK, then he kept the green side facing up; if he was struggling, he would turn the card over to the red side. This would allow the staff to realise that he needed help without the embarrassment for him, which is so important. What kid wants to stand up in the middle of class and be forced to explain that they are stuck in a ritual and need help? No, it's too difficult. Also, he was given 'Time Out' cards, so if he really felt he needed a break, to step outside of the class for ten minutes to calm down, then he would place that card on his desk and the teacher would nod that he could step outside. It is also helpful if your child is seated near the door, to allow for a less obvious exit.

Having an agreed quiet place to go to is a great idea; your child knows where to go and for how long, and the staff know where to find them. It all just takes the stress of having to explain out of your child's day, and allows them to focus on the important issue of getting an education.

If your child has problems with deadlines, as our son has, then homework tasks and tasks in class that need to be completed before the class ends can be a source of extreme stress. Now, we know we shouldn't ever be giving in to OCD but, we can only do one thing at a time. If the ERP task that week is something else, then it's perfectly OK to make a plan where your child is allowed additional time, or a deadline is not set for the work. Deadlines also come in the form of getting to class on time, or to school on time, or eating lunch in the allotted time, so all of these things can be affected by this ritual. Our son was allowed extended deadlines when he needed them and was definitely never disciplined for being late. Well, that's not to say that if he was late for a reason other than OCD he wouldn't be disciplined; if he was messing around, for example, he would be treated the same as any other student of course, but, if he was stuck in a ritual, then the staff knew that this was something he couldn't help and not something he was doing on purpose.

It's also helpful if your child's classes can be arranged as much as possible to be with their friends as this does help to give your child confidence, so sitting with friends whenever they can is good.

Finally, try and have your child's school nominate one person that your child can go to if they need to. This person should build a relationship with your child so they never feel alone, and always know that there is someone in the school who understands and can be trusted.

TIPS

★ You must communicate with the school. Explain clearly what your child requires. Develop a relationship and get them on your side.

★ If you feel the school isn't doing enough, tell them.

★ If they don't listen, seek advice from your local education authority.

★ Ask your child's therapist to get involved in drawing up a plan to help your child access school.

★ Changes in school could affect your child more than others. Ask the school for preparation time before any changes are implemented.

★ If your child's OCD is affecting their performance, explain this to the school. Homework may not be completed due to OCD making a child feel it's not 'right'. OCD may mean a child is often late for class due to repeated rituals, they may appear to day-dream, may fidget, or perform rituals in class, for example. The child should never be punished for this. Make a plan with the school for how this will be handled.

★ If this doesn't work, and your child stops attending school, you did your best. Regroup – the field of conflict may have changed, but the battle rages on.

★ Find a school that has a sympathetic approach to mental illness.

★ Ensure the school has adequate staff to cater for your child's needs.

☆ Ensure the school communicates all information with all staff that may work with your child.

☆ Watch out for bullying; your child may be more vulnerable than others.

☆ School isn't just for an academic education; it will give your child so much more if it's right. Strive to keep them in school.

CHAPTER 6

The Changing Nature of OCD

You know that fairground game where you have a big hammer and you have to hit the moles, or aliens or various other things that pop up and down, as fast as you can? One pops up on the right, you smash it, then one immediately pops up on the left, and you smash it, then another pops up in the middle...and so on? It's manic and you don't know where the next one will pop up, so you have to be prepared. That's what OCD has been like for us. Just when we think we've beaten one obsession...up pops another to fill its place.

In the beginning, I thought that his obsessions were his obsessions and that was what we were dealing with. Not so. For example, our son was obsessed with a collection of small figurines that he had had for years. They were characters from a cartoon show he used to like; he had eight of them. They were placed in a certain spot on his shelf, in a semi-circle and absolutely were not to be touched. If one of them was even slightly out place, he would become extremely anxious because he was 'told' by his OCD that I would die if they were moved.

Then, as part of his ERP therapy, he moved them. It was amazing to see him take charge of that obsession, and deal with the resulting anxiety so bravely. After the anxiety died down, which it always does if you don't do a ritual around it, he felt liberated. What a moment – triumph! He gave the figures to his little brother and we were delighted.

A couple of days later, I noticed something a little odd. His clothes were in a soaking pile in the corner of the bathroom. He'd had a shower and his clothes were soaked, as if he'd gone in the shower fully clothed. I didn't say anything that day, but watched for the next time he showered, and there it was again, soaking clothes. What was this now?

So, I asked him, 'Darling, why are your clothes soaking wet?' He got that shifty look about him and said, 'I'm sorry, I had to go in the shower with my clothes on.' 'Why?' I asked. 'Or you'd die.'

Brilliant. Another uninvited guest to evict. I thought we'd smashed that mole, but another one just popped up.

The problem was, while he was working very hard with his ERP, confronting fears and trying to beat them, he was still doing rituals. So, if he listened to a particular song that triggered his repeating compulsion, instead of repeating, he would count, or make the sign of the cross, or rock back and forth (while counting). Although he wasn't repeating words like OCD wanted and it was progress, he was still doing rituals to manage the anxiety. That just fuels OCD. The idea is to learn that the anxiety will go down on its own, and you won't learn that if you keep doing rituals, even if they're different rituals to the one you would normally do.

At this point, let me take you back to therapy and let you know what was going on. As you've read, our son was accepted for treatment by the Maudsley and he was allocated a therapist who would work with him to solve this problem. Enter Dr Amita Jassi. From the moment I met her, my confidence in therapy grew tenfold. This was a lady with a plan.

At our first session, she presented us with a workbook, filled with information, tasks and above all, direction. No more talking and trying to figure it out; this was a manual to stop OCD in its tracks. All children being treated at the Maudsley use it. It works. It was a revelation to me to see something so clear, so focused. I felt overwhelming relief that these people clearly knew what they were doing and they could help our son. It was like the difference between taking my car to a knowledgeable friend to see if he could figure out why my car wasn't working, and then taking it to a specialist garage, where they did a diagnostic test and told me, 'This is what it is, and this is how we fix it.' For the first time in a long time, I could see a solution. And...she knew Jedi mind tricks.

The first session was at the Maudsley clinic in London and our son was in a right state. He refused to speak, refused to cooperate, he hated us all and stated very clearly that none of this would work. Within five minutes, he was speaking to Amita. Within 15 minutes he was going for a walk on his own with Amita, leaving behind two open-mouthed parents. At the end of the session he announced he'd like to stop for a burger on the way home.

We were going to have a therapy session every week, and we had homework to do in between. The first week, it centred around understanding what anxiety is, how it works, the physical effects it has on you and why our body has anxiety in the first place. No mention of cutting down rituals or anything like that, just education about the symptoms.

The second session the following week, and our son was in a worse state. You see, OCD doesn't like it when you challenge it. It doesn't want you to do anything that might make it lose its power over you. Dr Jassi proved a significant threat to my son's OCD, and it kicked back. It was very scary, and you could be forgiven for thinking that things were getting worse but, actually, this is perfectly normal and common. It doesn't mean things are deteriorating, it just means the real fight has begun.

Bring it on.

The train trip to London was fraught. Our son was terrified. OCD was filling his head with ideas about train crashes and terrorist attacks. Also, London had only recently endured the riots, so OCD was screaming that this was the most dangerous place on earth to go, and something awful was bound to happen. He hadn't slept at all and refused food.

When we got to the Maudsley, we were all drained, and the thought of therapy on top of that was exhausting, plus we had to go through it all again to get back home. Drawing reserves from your toes becomes second nature, though, and I always had the headmistress in my head to fall back on.

Before we went into therapy, our son was weighed by one of the psychiatrists and he had lost some weight, which wasn't a surprise given he was hardly eating, but was a huge concern. He was quite underweight.

Then, we sat with Amita and carried on with the workbook but our son was so involved with rituals that he started off not hearing much. At no point, though, did I feel anything other than calm acceptance that this had all been seen before by Amita. Her reassurance and unfazed approach was like balm to my nerves, and to our son's as he gradually came out of his shell over the hour.

Session 3. OCD was bringing out the big guns. This time it told our son that he shouldn't go to London for all the previous reasons, plus…he was convinced he would say something racist and offensive to Amita. You see, she is of Asian descent, and my son did have urges to say swear words and offensive comments that he sometimes was unable to resist. The thought of saying something racist was horrific to him. Racism of any kind is totally unacceptable to our family, and OCD knew it. He didn't say anything awful, of course, but he had to fight the urge strongly and was terrified of losing control. At the end of the session, it was discussed that we should begin confronting a fear or two.

As I said about ERP, the usual routine is to draw up a hierarchy of fears, then tackle them one by one, starting with the least scary and working your way up. In our son's case, however, we needed to address his food worries, because he was underweight and losing more all the time. The worry was, obviously, that he was very close to putting his physical health at serious risk. So, even though it was quite high on his hierarchy, we had to start there.

Some of our son's rituals around food were watching me prepare it, checking the food was properly cooked and checking sell by dates. His task the following week would be...Amita would bring some food. He would not see it prepared, he would not see the sell by date and he would not check to see if it was cooked. He would just eat some. And then, we would wait and see if his fears came true.

It sounds cruel, doesn't it? When you put it like that, it sounds really cruel but it's the only way an OCD sufferer will actually learn that their fears aren't real. They have to experiment and watch the outcome. There has to be proof and the only way to get proof is to try it out and see what happens.

So, that decided, off we went for the train ride home. Disaster. Sometimes, life just goes OCD's way and that day, it played right into its hands. We had to catch the tube to get back to Waterloo and there was a problem on the line, an accident, they said, and we got stuck. With other cancellations, the tube we were on became seriously congested, people packing themselves in like sardines, all pressed up against us. Our son was squashed between three people, who were coughing, some were from ethnic minorities, his face was pressed against a man's armpit…you can imagine. He fainted and so I had to hold him up while we made slow progress to Waterloo because we couldn't get off.

I stood there on the Bakerloo line, holding up my child, breathing into someone's armpit and thought, 'What have I done to deserve this? Was I Vlad the Impaler in a previous life?' I looked at the people around us, listening to iPods, staring blankly into space, they seemed like they were on a different planet. Their lives seemed so uncomplicated, it wasn't fair that my beautiful boy had to go through this nightmare. It wasn't fair that my whole family had to live like this, in this world of dangers and fears, of rituals and anxiety. Why should it have happened to us? Why couldn't it have happened to me, if it had to happen to one of us? Why this clever, kind boy who never hurt anybody in his life, who only wanted to look after his loved ones?

If I could take it from him I would but I can't, so, I can't go under to those thoughts. I have a right to feel them, of course, who wouldn't? But, if it's bad for the rest of us, it's a thousand times worse for him.

By the time Session 4 came round the following week, he was absolutely refusing to go. He was in such a state of panic on the morning of therapy, having a proper panic attack which, for my son, involves screaming, refusing to be touched and hitting out, we knew there was no way we could safely transport him to London.

So, I called the Maudsley to let them know, thinking that we were about to lose the game. I couldn't believe the response.

Not only did Amita tell me that this wasn't uncommon and she quite understood that the idea of confronting his food fears was totally overwhelming, she told me that this happens a lot; kids with OCD often can't get in to the clinic because of their various fears and, although they always try to see them in clinic as a preference, she was happy to come to us. To say I wanted to kiss her would not be an exaggeration.

So, after that, and for a few months, Amita would come out to us every other week, and have an hour's session on the phone in between. Our son didn't make much progress in terms of stopping his rituals, or easing his fears but he made huge progress with accepting what he had. Amita managed what I thought was the impossible. Our son actually said the words, 'I have OCD.'

One night, I went up to his room, as I do every night, to begin the process of calming him down enough so I can go to bed and get a little sleep. Some nights are OK, and only take a couple of hours, some nights are awful and take a lot longer. Persuading him into his pyjamas and encouraging him to lie down are all things that take quite a lot of effort, because they mark the start of the bedtime routine, and the knowledge that he has to try and get some sleep. I've learned that there's no point insisting over and over again that he does those things, all that makes him do is get more stressed. So, I talk about anything and everything. I spend most of the day thinking of things that we can talk about that night: things I've seen on the news, trivia quizzes for us to do, books I've read and my son's favourite game 'What's your Top 10...?' We start with one of those things each night, as I've found that distracting him from his constant ruminations makes OCD quieten down enough for my son to get through a bit. Some nights, even that doesn't work and I have to resort to desperate measures. I'll talk about what they are later, but please, don't judge me!

This particular night, I went into his room and he was in his usual place, kneeling on his bed on the floor (he's not 'allowed' to touch his real bed), wringing his hands and rocking to and fro. I went into my usual routine of bright chat, when he suddenly blurted out, 'Mummy, I know I've got OCD,' then threw himself into his pillows, burying his face away. I thought I'd heard him wrong. I couldn't believe that he had actually admitted it. Making a fuss is the worst thing I can do about anything with my son, so I calmly, as nonchalantly as I could, replied, 'I know, baby, it's rubbish, isn't it?' He turned his face towards me, a picture of fear and vulnerability and said, 'I don't want to be like this anymore.'

I can't tell you what a breakthrough that was. It meant that he accepted that his fears aren't real, they are due to a condition, and it doesn't really make sense. It didn't mean he didn't still want to do them, or that he wasn't terrified of stopping, but he began to see that there is another way to live your life, and that he didn't want to be like he was forever. He wanted to see his friends, go to school, eat, not spend all of his time doing rituals and being afraid. Breakthrough.

But we were still playing whack-a-mole because, although his ERP sessions with Amita were going ahead and he was really trying, he was still doing rituals so he wasn't learning that his anxiety will come down on its own. He was still depending on rituals to calm himself, which was a real shame because he was doing all the work of allowing his anxiety to climb up by doing something scary, but not getting the benefit from it, or any longer-term relief. So, one fear is confronted, another pops up in its place. And, so it goes.

The great thing about having someone like Dr Jassi involved, though, is that she has seen it all before. Something that, to me, is quite shocking, is totally normal in her world, she's been working with kids with Extreme OCD for years, and nothing fazes her. With that support, and calm reassurance, it is so much easier to get through the days.

TIPS

★ OCD will often change approach, and new compulsions will arise – look out for changes.

★ If your child is scared of doing something, the best way to handle that is to do it!

★ Don't be afraid of your child's fear – remember that it's OCD; the danger isn't real.

★ Learn what anxiety is, why it makes you feel awful, how it affects you physically, then teach your child. The more they understand what's happening to them, the easier it is to fight it.

★ Encourage your child to see if their anxiety will come down on its own without doing rituals.

★ Start slowly! Don't start at the scariest thing, choose something less scary and build on that.

★ ERP sessions will make your child more anxious at first – this does not mean they aren't working – it means they are.

★ Make sure you tell your child often how brave they are. OCD will damage your child's self-esteem and make it even harder to stand up to it.

* Regularly praise any effort to confront OCD, even if it doesn't work. Just trying is extremely hard.

* Never tell your child off for doing a ritual. Ask why they felt they couldn't resist and talk about how you can help.

* Therapy is exhausting for you, too. Make sure you recharge in your favourite way.

* If you feel like screaming – go scream into your pillow by all means, feel free!

CHAPTER 7

Tears, Tantrums and Other Outbursts

One of the hardest things about OCD is the anxiety. People don't realise that, along with the rituals, comes fear that just won't quit. And, along with the fear, comes emotional outbursts on a grand scale.

Funnily enough, the rituals aren't the worst culprit for this in our house. The biggest culprits for anxiety are the horrible images and urges, including the feeling of things just not being 'right' and the actual obsessions. The rituals, or compulsions, make the anxiety last longer, but it's the original obsession that makes it explode in the first place.

Our son gets images of Charles Manson. Don't ask me where this comes from, it's another of OCD's great mysteries. He must have seen that infamous picture of him in court with that demented look on his face and the swastika carved into his forehead and OCD thought, 'That man is going to come in the night and kill you all'. He has images of Charles Manson coming into his room at night and cutting his throat (my son's, not his own, unfortunately), or creeping into my room and raping me. Graphic, awful images, sparing him no detail, torturing him with worse and worse fates for us all.

No matter how many times I explain that said Mr Manson is a crumbly old man of 78 now, in a locked cell, in a maximum security prison, in America and if he should manage to (i) escape prison (ii) get to an airport (iii) fly 12 hours to England (iv) get on a train from Heathrow and (v) get a taxi from the train station to our quiet suburban cul-de-sac, somehow managing to break in at the end of it and climb the stairs to our rooms...after all that...I'm pretty confident I could take the old geezer.

No matter how many times I explain this (once every night, and once only)...still old Charlie haunts our son.

He's the reason my son won't sleep at night. The reason he makes the sign of the cross almost all night, the reason he taps me (when he can catch me) or goes in the shower with his clothes on. It's not all Mr Manson, our son also worries I will get cancer or be raped by some other person, but Charles is the star of the show. So, he's the obsession. It's that that causes the anxiety, and the anxiety causes the rituals. Then the rituals fuel the anxiety, and the anxiety fuels the obsession. Round and round it goes. Short of challenging Charles Manson to a no-holds-barred wrestling match, though, that obsession is very hard to challenge.

So, the only way to stop it, is to break the cycle somewhere else. He's obsessed with Manson, that's hard to stop, and you can't tell your body not to be anxious. The only link in the chain that can be changed are the rituals that fuel the anxiety. Stop them, and the cycle is disrupted, the obsession isn't fed, and it fades. Easy, right? Unfortunately...the anxiety might not be based upon reality, but it is as real as if Charles Manson really was standing at the bottom of our stairs, chopping knife in hand, intent on murder.

Getting through to our son when he's anxious is very hard. OCD is so active in his mind that he can't focus on what I'm saying. He paces his room, hyperventilating, wringing his hands, his pulse rate increases, he breaks out in a cold sweat and he won't allow any physical contact, so no mummy cuddles – thought they'd always make everything OK. He shouts at me, has even thrown things at me and, as things escalate, has trashed his room, hidden in cupboards, locked himself in the bathroom and physically attacked me. Mostly, he wants to be left alone, but a lot of the time, it's not safe to do that, so I have to take what's thrown at me...literally.

If I can, if it's safe to do so, I do give him ten minutes to himself. Often this will help and when I go back in, he's a little more in control. The real problems begin when he's in this state, and I need him to do something.

Quite often, our son is terrified of coming downstairs for his lesson with Mr A. If I let him not come down, though, then it will be even harder for him the next day. I can't let OCD have that. So, there have been times when I've had to physically get him downstairs and in the same room as Mr A at least. These are the times when he has hit out at me, even headbutted me once, not because he is a violent child, he was just a terrified child. He was in literal fight or flight mode, and as I wouldn't let him flee, he fought!

Those days are hard. Not only are they physically exhausting because he is really strong when he's panicking, but they are mentally and emotionally draining. Nothing prepares you for the shock of being hit by your child. Even understanding why only softens the blow a little.

When things have calmed down, and I'm sitting alone with a cup of tea, face stinging, those are the times I've cried the most. Seeing him so afraid, knowing that I had forced him into that, and then seeing him so remorseful afterwards, so distraught at what he'd done, is absolutely dreadful.

I remember chubby little arms held up at me, shouting, 'Mummy, up! Mummy, up!' and scooping him up, breathing in the smell of him, snuggling into his soft little neck. Those tiny fingers that used to grip my hand so hard, that morning-cosy body cuddling up to me in bed. Picking him up from pre-school, seeing his face light up when he sees me, running to me on too slow legs that wanted to fly but could only waddle.

My precious little boy, beloved and special to me. My sensitive, darling child. This bruise on my cheek doesn't belong to him, those hands that left it, not his. This is the cheek for butterfly kisses, and those are the hands of a million blown 'I Love You's'.

How *dare* this awful condition make my son do this? It makes me so *angry*. There should never have been those feelings between us, those scenes. Violence should never have been in our home, would never have been in our home, without this vile thing.

It's not him, though. It's OCD. Remembering that has been my sanity, and the only thing I've had to hold on to. I picture his OCD as a sly, shadowing thing, a creature of whispers and dark corners. A creature of secrets and smoke. It'd make a great character in Harry Potter, my son's OCD would. What I wouldn't give for a wand and a well-timed Expelliarmus spell!

So, yes, anxiety is a problem. The only advice I can give you is, remember it's not your child, stay calm and don't allow your child's panic to panic you. The symptoms of the fear are real, but the danger is not, so you have nothing to protect them from. As long as you know they are safe, let the anxiety come down on its own. It will in the end. It always does.

OCD and the big P

Add puberty into the equation and mood swings make for an interesting addition to the OCD mix. Sometimes, it's hard to distinguish between what's OCD and what's just a stroppy teenager throwing a paddy, or being lazy. Teenagers don't like to be told what to do by their parents, they challenge boundaries and begin to exercise their independence. All this is normal but, when my son leaves a wet towel on the floor for the umpeenth time, you can't help but wonder, is this another OCD thing?

Now, to my knowledge, our son has never blamed OCD for things that are not OCD. But, he has said things are not OCD when they are, so my psychic mother powers have to come into play and it's down to instinct again. I think I know our son pretty well, but OCD has turned him into quite a convincing little liar at times and he has sworn to my face that certain things aren't OCD, when they clearly are. OCD likes secrets, and my son, being a teenager, can't be bothered to go through 'another boring therapy session' (sic) if he tells me that something's OCD so, he gets stroppy, moody teenager on me and slams from the room. Some of it is OCD, some of it is attitude.

It's hard to isolate the attitude and put boundaries in place. I mean, he is still our son, not just OCD, and there are rules in the house, such as tidying up after yourself and having respect. Sometimes, the anxiety comes across as stroppiness and I have to put my foot down, even though I know where it's coming from. I think it's important he's treated like a normal child, he is a normal child; and it's still my job as a mother to guide him and shape him into a productive, compassionate man. Allowing him to speak to me in a rude way is not acceptable, regardless of the reasons for it. OCD or no OCD, it's not OK to be disrespectful. Of course, this rule has to be modified if he really is in a state and I know he's panicking; he's always very sorry after that without me having to tell him but, if it's just general anxiety, it's not allowed.

Between OCD and hormones…I'm surprised there are any doors left on hinges in our house!

I'm really lucky that our son and I have a very open relationship. We talk about anything and everything under the sun, so he mostly feels able to tell me how he's feeling. A large problem for him is: it's all so confusing! I remember puberty (yes, I do, it wasn't that long ago, you know), and clearly recall how upside down everything felt. One minute I was happy, then I was crying, then I was spitting fire at someone for looking at me funny, then I was crying again. Pubescent kids are a mess. It's not pretty.

OCD is really confusing, too. All the intrusive thoughts flying around in their heads, adding to the confusion, I really can't imagine how hard that must be. So, that has led to a natural step back for our son from me. It's normal, and healthy, for a young person to gradually move away from their parents' influence. They learn to think for themselves, trust their own judgement, become independent. Our son has struggled with this; it's caused a lot of conflict inside himself. He feels the natural urge to assert his independence, he wants more space, more privacy, but then OCD jumps in and becomes afraid of that independence because he doesn't trust himself, and is afraid of the world, so he moves closer again.

I've noticed that he has become quite resentful of this. He wants both to still be protected by me and to be independent. His OCD makes him believe that if he is out in the world on his own, something very bad will happen. His puberty makes him believe that if he is stuck with me for the rest of his life, that is the bad thing that will happen!

So, I am both hero and villain in this picture. He'll grow out of it, though, won't he? I'm reliably informed that in about 35 years or so he'll definitely stop blaming me for everything!

Why me? There, I said it

Then there are the other tantrums, mine. Oh yes, I've said you need to be calm, you should never show you're stressed or anxious yourself and all of that is true. Sometimes, though, I can't help it. Sometimes I'm just so tired that I have no patience. It doesn't happen often but it does happen. Days when I've counted to ten so many times, gone for a walk around the garden so often I've created a track, but still the stress continues and, I crack. There are only so many times I can say, 'I've answered that question' or rise above being yelled at before it starts to wear me down. I'm only human, after all.

While OCD seems to have taken over our lives, there is still the usual stress of ordinary life to contend with. Things like finances play a large part in our everyday stress. I used to work full time and brought in a good wage. I loved my career and was good at what I did. Now, I'm a full-time carer and, although I know and accept that this is where I'm needed and this is my priority, not having that income or that personal fulfilment is hard.

There are days when I do whine to myself, 'Why me?' like a child and lie in bed dreading what's to come. When my life comes into sharp focus and I think, 'How the hell did this happen?' Just because OCD has decided to honour us with its presence, it doesn't mean I'm not still the person I always was. I was never your earth mother type. I adore my kids but am not a bake sale and home craft projects kind of girl. I'm more your loud music and new handbags woman. I like socialising, I like dancing, I like eating out and going to the movies. I like high heels and getting my hair done.

I've never been the most patient person, so dealing with OCD and the level of patience it requires has been a massive struggle. Don't be fooled by my exterior calm or apparent control of the situation; most of the time, inside, I'm lying on the floor kicking my legs and screaming like a two-year-old. It's not fair on my son, but it's not fair on me either. I didn't choose this career, I didn't feel a calling to work with this illness, I have no skills either natural or taught. I'm just a normal mother, in a crazy situation, doing her best. My best isn't always good enough, because I'm not perfect. It never affects our son, except for the times when my patience is gone and I snap at him, but we always talk about it and he understands. I'm quite open with him, with both of my kids, that I'm not perfect. I make mistakes, as everybody does. It's hard to admit that. I'm quite ashamed of myself, to have those dark thoughts in my head. I really feel they shouldn't be there. Do other mothers feel this way?

Don't get me wrong, I'm never cruel or nasty. It's just that sometimes I'm not as patient as I know I should be. Especially at mealtimes. By the end of the day, I am tired. Our youngest son is home from school and we all sit and eat together. Our eldest son, as I've said before, has an obsession about vomiting. This means he finds it hard to eat, because he fears the food may make him vomit, for various reasons. Mostly, he feels that if he has nothing in his stomach, there's nothing to throw up, and feeling full, the sensation of having food in his stomach, makes him very anxious.

Four mealtimes out of seven, we get through it without too much drama. The other three are carnage. I watch our son's head drop lower and lower. I see him begin to rock back and forth slightly, I can hear the deep breathing, see him moving food around his plate and I know, here we go. I start off speaking to him about anything, but he usually ignores me; he's too deep in conversation with OCD in his head. I speak more loudly to get his attention, and he snaps at me. I tell him he must eat his dinner as, more often than not, this is the only meal he's had all day. He shouts at me. He refuses to eat. He screams that it's disgusting. He pushes his food away and flatly refuses.

Meanwhile, our six-year-old is watching this, and also putting his fork down, saying the food is disgusting. This is my trigger point. I look at our son and say, in a low voice, that his brother is copying him and could he please consider the affect he is having? He says he doesn't care, and all I care about is his brother. He tells me he hates me. Our six-year-old rises to his brother's defence, he hates me too now. I'm being screamed at by two children...that's the point when my patience can crack.

I know, I know, it's not my son, it's OCD. I know. I should calmly offer our six-year-old the chance to eat elsewhere so that I can handle the situation away from him, but it's not that easy and I don't want my six-year-old to feel he is being left alone because of his brother. So, I tell my eldest son not to speak to me like that, and I get involved in an argument with him, which is exactly what he wants me to do because then he can blow up, deflecting the attention away from eating, and slam from the room in righteous anger. Leaving his plate of dinner behind.

I know this is what he's doing, and a lot of the time I am able to rise above it and stay calm, but I'd be lying to you if I didn't admit that sometimes, he pushes the right buttons in the right order and I react. Mostly, it's the grinding repetition, every day exactly the same as the one before, the same fears of the same things, the same words said at the same times, the same fights and the same encouragements...the suffocating boredom of it. His routines make him feel safe, but they make me feel trapped. Am I a bad mother? I hope not. I'm the best mother I can be, but in my eyes nothing will ever be good enough for my boys, least of all me.

My tantrums don't only affect the kids, though. Mostly, they are taken out on my long-suffering partner. When your child has something like OCD, it has an impact on your relationship and I have thrown some terrible tantrums his way. Usually, it's not over my day, or how I'm feeling, it's over dirty washing left on the floor or washing up not put away properly. It's just a vent but the pressure has to come out somewhere, and it comes out there.

I really feel for him. He works long hours and doesn't see the worst of our son often, so it must be hard for him to relate to how I'm feeling. Especially when I say, 'I'm fine', complete with dramatic hair swishes, clearly indicating that I'm not fine at all. Most of the time, he's bewildered by me, and I think he's also a little afraid of me sometimes, like he feels he should throw his hat in the door first to see if the coast is clear. It's not fair on him; he really is the most wonderful man. How he puts up with me, I'll never know. He must wonder where the woman he met has gone. I wonder that, too. I used to be confident and independent. Now, I'm tired, stressed, frustrated and my self-confidence is a distant memory, lost in the isolation. I'm dependent on him financially and, although he has no problem with that, I have. I hate being dependent; it makes me feel like a burden.

Phew! What a melting pot of emotion! I have to say, though, that most of the time, all these emotions are handled. I mean, you just get on with it, don't you? What choice have you got? I can't take to my bed, can I? There are people who need me, and I can't let them down.

Inspiration vs exasperation

OCD has to be one of the most frustrating conditions around. A lot of the time I feel as if there is an actual brick wall strapped to my head, and every time I move, I bang my head against it.

We do have good days and they mean everything. A day when he's smiling, and laughing. A day when he comes and looks for something to eat, or sits downstairs with us and is relaxed. A day when he chats to me and his personality shines through. Yes, they are perfect days. How can I explain then, that these perfect days, infrequent though they are, are overshadowed for me by the knowledge that it won't last? I'm too scared to be optimistic, because I have built my hopes up so many times and OCD has shimmied sideways with a quick one-two, and I realise that we haven't moved forward that much, we've kind of moved sideways.

Look, he's going to school now, its part time and he doesn't go into lessons that much and he often comes home early or doesn't go in, but he goes. He sleeps on his bed. He knows he has OCD and his confidence is better. These are improvements, I know they are and I feel just awful for thinking, 'Two years of therapy, a hospital stay, and that's *it*? I mean, seriously, that's *it*?' I can't be happy about that. I can't feel as if we're winning. He's 13, he should be thinking about a career, not struggling to leave his room. Compare him with another boy his age and…really…come on now…that's *it*?

We go into a therapy session and I explain the kind of week we've had, and the therapist responds by reminding me of his achievements. Other parents celebrate academic success: straight As, sports achievements, dancing prowess, musical talents. We celebrate when he eats a yoghurt, or touches a door handle, or flushes the toilet. Or sleeps. I know these are achievements, no one knows better than me how hard he has worked to achieve those things. I don't need to be reminded of them. I don't want a cheerleader, I want an acknowledgement of reality, and a plan to change it. That's what I need to hear.

I know what they're trying to do; it's really difficult for them and I don't blame them at all. I just find it very frustrating that we seem to be pretending that this is acceptable. Now, our son is always present in these meetings, and I am in no way suggesting that we should be anything other than fiercely optimistic in front of him. I do feel that time should be dedicated to actually hearing what the reality of the situation is from the people living it, however. How can we plan our attack if they don't have all the facts? A stubborn determination to focus on the positives is great, and for our son, vital. Behind the scenes, though, I feel there should be a little more honesty.

I'm sorry if I'm painting a bleak picture here. Most cases of OCD are resolved, it can be beaten. It's just that the road feels so long sometimes and the wins are so small along the way. Collectively, the wins add up, and in the end, you get to the finish line. Take them individually and it can feel like running a marathon by taking only one step per day. The progress is easy to overlook, then one day, I suppose, you look back and see that you've come a long way, it just didn't feel like it at the time.

So, we soldier on. One foot in front of the other, one day at a time, grabbing the highs and trying not to slide into the lows. My mum used to say, 'Don't look at the big picture' and she was right. We look at the little bit of the picture that's right in front of us and deal with that. If we stood back and looked at the big picture too often, we'd spend all our time standing still, trying to take it all in. That's the best piece of advice I can give you. Don't look at the big picture unless you really have to. Take things one step at a time, deal with each issue as it arises, don't look too far ahead, or too far behind. If you deal with each issue as a piece of the puzzle, one day you'll stand back and see a picture starting to emerge, and one day, it really will be complete.

TIPS

★ Stay calm – recognise if you're getting stressed and take a few minutes out.

★ Don't put everything down to OCD – but don't overlook OCD.

* ✶ Rules are rules – your child should still abide by the rules of your home. Make time for your partner.

* ✶ Don't hide what's happening – ask for help if you need it.

* ✶ Ease up on yourself – you're doing your best.

* ✶ Remember – it's OCD – not your child – that's the problem.

* ✶ Anxiety will pass – it will not harm your child.

* ✶ When you're confident and calm – your child will feel safer.

* ✶ Don't look at the big picture.

CHAPTER 8

The Rest of the Family

It's easy to get so involved with your child who has OCD, that you overlook other siblings. Not that you don't give them enough attention or anything, but sometimes, you forget, in your day to day, how different life is for them, too.

Our youngest son is not being brought up the way any of the other children in our family have been raised. He is loved and gets a lot of attention but he rarely gets to go out with us all together as a family. And, if we do all go out together, usually my attention is taken up with keeping my eldest son as calm as possible or dealing with his panic attacks if things get too hard. I'm always on edge, so my youngest never sees me totally relax and have fun with him the way my eldest did at his age, before OCD arrived and changed everything. He's never known anything different, so it's hard to say what kind of impact that has on him but it's not what I wanted for him at all. I want our youngest to know how much I enjoy him, but we rarely get the opportunity outside of the house, and even inside the house, it's not easy.

Our youngest has learned that as his brother isn't well, he gets attention for that. There are often times when I have to drop everything to deal with something that's come up with OCD, and can't wait. Our whole house is affected by OCD, and my youngest son is used to the bizarre nature of how we live our lives. He is used to his brother screaming at mealtimes, he is used to his brother refusing to go into an upstairs room with an open window, or fleeing the kitchen from a knife, or weeing in a bucket at night. What difficult things for a six-year-old to get used to. Little kids are amazing, though, in what they accept with a shrug, but I wish he didn't have to have those things around him.

One of the things our six-year-old finds very difficult to accept is his brother not wanting to sit next to him, or flinching if he gets too near. He never gets hugs or kisses from his brother, even though my oldest six-year-old is very tactile and wants them all the time. He'll go over to his brother with his arms wide for a hug and my eldest son will look horror stricken and back away. Sometimes he will allow his younger brother to hug him, though, but never hugs back and stands very stiffly for a few seconds before moving quickly away. From our six-year-old's point of view, he takes this personally. He is expressing love for his brother, who he does adore, but his brother seems to be saying that the feeling is not returned. I've explained to our six-year-old over and over again about OCD and why this is happening but it's a hard concept to grasp and, as he is superhero obsessed, he just wants to bash OCD and make it leave his brother alone. I wish it were that easy, and how lovely it is to have such a black-and-white view.

Our youngest is a lovely, sweet boy when it's just me and his brother is upstairs but, the second he comes downstairs, you can see the change come over him. He knows that, if his brother is feeling bad, I will talk to him, and my six-year-old desperately wants to keep my attention with him. So, he'll start being cheeky or doing things he knows he shouldn't, because that will make me stop talking to his brother, and focus back on him.

It's a perennial problem, sibling rivalry, not exclusive to OCD, but OCD makes it harder to do the things that will help the problem, like having rules about one-on-one time. If I sit down to read with my youngest, which I often do, and my eldest comes downstairs obviously anxious, and says that he feels sick, I have to stop what I'm doing. If I don't, then my eldest will get even more anxious and I will still have to stop what I'm doing, but it will last for longer so I won't be able to get back to the book and spend some time with my youngest. I do try not to let it interfere, but OCD is a demanding beast and you can't ignore it for long. It's hard to concentrate on reading when your other child is pacing up and down in front of you, crying and saying he's not going to eat or drink. What can I do?

So, our youngest then fights back by trying to rip the book or throwing it at me, or something along those lines, and I have to ask him to wait just two minutes while I talk to his brother. He doesn't want me to do that, so he will actually rip the book or scream at me. Then he gets a warning, and he carries on, then he ends up on the naughty spot. It's awful because I know why he's doing it, but there's nothing I can do about it.

I try to make sure I have at least one hour every day to spend alone with my youngest. We watch a movie or read a book or play a game, but an hour isn't enough, and it isn't always uninterrupted.

Our youngest knows that his brother has his school lessons at home, or is only at school part time on a good day, and also wants to stay at home with me. He sees this as preferential treatment and thinks it's very unfair. If I put myself in his shoes, I'm sure I would have protested loudly when I was his age, too. It seems like heaven to him that his brother only has one hour of school a day, in our dining room, he doesn't have to do lessons he doesn't like, and he gets to stay at home, watch TV or sleep the rest of the time. At his age, he doesn't understand about opportunities missed, or his brother's loneliness and boredom; he just sees him with me all the time…and he's jealous.

Then, there's the problem of him hero worshipping his older brother. You know what kids are like, usually they just want to be like their older sibling. I know I did. I was the youngest and thought my older sister was the coolest person on the planet and wanted to wear all her clothes and listen to all her music. She hated it, but she was the person I modelled myself on. My role model.

When your youngest child's role model is behaving in a way that you would rather wasn't copied, you're in trouble. Our youngest child gets the occasional quirk that he's learned from his brother. He also doesn't like to be dirty (that's when he thinks about it – he's fine with dirt when he's too busy having fun) and he is also a bit wary of knives. Having seen his brother's reaction, he thinks there must be something to be scared of. This learned behaviour is frustrating and very hard to prevent. As I said, our son's fears are very real to him and his reaction is impossible to hide. I understand that the danger isn't real, but a six-year-old is scared.

He's also scared by all the shouting and screaming that comes with his brother being anxious. It must be hard for a little one to see someone so out of control. He hasn't seen any of the really bad panic attacks, but he has seen enough of the medium ones to be cautious. I try to compensate for this with lots of cuddles and explanations about what is happening. We are very open with him about what OCD is, and why it makes his brother react the way he sometimes does. Educating him about it is the only way I can think of to help him process the things he sometimes sees and hears, and I'm sure it has helped.

But...and here's the kicker...he has told me that he wishes he had OCD.

I've read that it's common for kids to wish they had a medical condition suffered by a sibling, because they only interpret the positives of lots of attention and no school; they don't understand the negatives a medical condition can have on your life. How awful to feel envious of a medical condition. He doesn't mean that he wants to be ill; I think he's just envious of the attention he feels his older brother gets. He wishes his brother's OCD would come and live in him, so that he wouldn't have to go to school, and has told me a few times that he has OCD.

Now, he is educated enough about this condition to fake it, and he has given me some very worrying moments when he has done something, or said something, that I've thought, 'What was that?' and then he does it again and again, finally claiming that he can't help it, he has to do it. Then he tells me he has OCD and it's not his fault, and I know he's attention seeking. That and the fact that he usually 'has' to do something he's not allowed to do, but really wants to, like eating another biscuit or jumping on my bed!

It's been hard to deal with because experts can see a genetic pre-disposition to the condition. This means that a person may be more likely to develop an anxiety condition due to a genetic disposition to be sensitive to worry and anxiety. My nephew has a less severe case of OCD and has had treatment for it, with a successful outcome. So, I watch my youngest son like a hawk for signs, especially now he's at the age when his brother really started to show symptoms.

The thing I've noticed the most are signs of stress. You know I said about my worst trigger point being mealtimes? Well, I've noticed our six-year-old showing signs of being affected by that, too. We sit down to dinner and he starts talking. And he talks and he talks, he talks about everything under the sun, sometimes he's just saying words that don't make a complete sentence and, no matter how many times he's asked to eat his food and take a break, he carries on talking. It's like he's trying to hold the moment, as if he feels like, if he keeps talking, then OCD won't be able to get a word in. I understand that feeling, and it's a worrying sign of how he is affected by the stress of living with OCD. I confess: I haven't found a solution to that problem. I can only carry on trying my hardest not to get stressed myself in those situations, and hope that helps him.

He is my second child, but actually my first without a medical condition, and I think that shapes how I parent him in many ways. The contrast between his needs and his older brother's are vast, and sometimes I think I may trivialise his needs because they just aren't as desperate, or worrying. I'm actually doing all of this for the first time with him, kind of making it up as I go along.

I worry about parenting him in the context of his brother's condition, rather than taking him as an individual. He's quite a robust child, well, he certainly is compared to his brother and that's the thing. Is he really a robust child, or is it just that he seems that way given my other experience? At the moment, he's too young to really vocalise any feelings of discontent, he will rather just behave badly and that's my cue that he needs some attention. I do try. It's so hard to know if I'm getting it right, I suppose time will tell. As he gets older, I'm sure he'll let me know. In the meantime, I try to let him know how loved he is and hope that is enough. I know that OCD is robbing us both of his normal childhood. I'd love to be the mother I imagined I would be, playing in the park, lots of fun, but it's just not been possible and I've had to modify and adjust things according to OCD.

The thing he likes best are his friends, and he has loads. So, I throw our home open to them. It's hard for me to get him out, so I bring them here. He loves that, and it does wonders for his confidence. Welcoming his friends, giving them treats, these are things you would do for an only child, and I feel that in some ways, he is. I definitely have to do things very differently between them, and I don't want our youngest to miss out on everything.

Small things bother me. Maybe they're not small. To our shame, he can't ride a bike yet or swim. When his brother was his age, he could do both of those things, but we just haven't done it with him. Oh, that's awful. It's not that we can't be bothered, it's just that getting out to the park is difficult, and we're always so tired that we've put it off. Poor kid. We do lots of other things with him, his dad takes him to movies or out for the day, but I'm never there. It's the normal things, the things you do as part of your day, that have suffered. I read with him a lot, and we draw together, but most of the time he spends with me is inside the house, and he is such a rough and tumble little boy, I know I'm missing out on a whole load of fun with him, and he's missing out on sharing that with me. He doesn't know any different but I can't say how it's shaping him.

How I wish things were different. This isn't what I expected, and it's not what any of us deserve.

He is loved, and he knows it. He gets love by the bucket full, and I confess, he does get very spoilt with material things.

I know I compensate for the things he's missing out on by buying him toys, and I know that they aren't compensating, but I feel I have to do something. What he really wants is time, but I don't always have that to give, so he gets a toy instead. I know it's wrong, but I am yet to think of a way around it. We don't have people on hand to care for our oldest son while we focus on our youngest; if we did, we'd arrange to do that regularly so that we could share ourselves out a little more fairly, but we are largely on our own. I can't split myself in two. It's tough.

On the positive side, he is doing very well at school, has lots of friends and good manners. So, we must be doing something right, mustn't we? More luck than design I think, but I'll take my comfort where I can.

TIPS

★ Try to make time for your other children.

★ Don't beat yourself up if things aren't the way you planned. Just do your best.

★ Be a tag team – sometimes doing things apart is the best you can do.

★ It's quality not quantity that matters most – make the time you do spend with your other children count.

★ Understand tantrums. OCD can be hard to compete with – your child may be afraid of being overlooked.

★ Explain what's going on to your other children. Involve them. This will help them understand that it's not their fault.

★ Love. Kisses. Hugs. There can never be enough.

Other family relationships

I read a beautiful quote once, a long time ago: 'A child isn't raised by their parents, it's raised by the whole village'. Your village is your whole extended family, and community. OCD has changed our village, so they aren't able to be as involved as they are with the rest of the children that live in it. Aunts, uncles and cousins don't enjoy the same easy time with us that they used to. They're all very supportive and understanding; it's not that they avoid us at all, but get-togethers aren't what they used to be.

Mostly it's because our son finds it very difficult to socialise, even with close family. He misses them and tries hard from time to time to spend time with them, but is always very withdrawn and anxious when they're around. There's always an atmosphere of slight concern. We'll all be talking but I've got one eye on him, or half my mind upstairs with him if he stays in his room away from them, as he often does. There are frequent looks across the table between his dad and me, as we communicate, 'Have you checked him?' and 'He's not good upstairs', then one of us will disappear to make sure he's OK.

A lot of the time, our youngest son and his dad will go to family get-togethers alone, it's just easier that way. Our eldest is often so anxious at the thought of being in someone else's house, we know he won't enjoy it. He's usually prepared to go, though, he feels guilty at making us stop doing things because of him but it really does have to be a special occasion to make us think of putting him through that.

We've tried doing it more often, and making him go, using the ERP train of thought that the more he does it and learns that nothing bad happens, the easier it gets, and it should work that way. With our son, though, it hasn't. Every time we did it, it was the same as the previous time, I expect because he was doing rituals to stop bad things happening, so his belief that rituals are the only thing standing between him and danger didn't diminish.

It's a shame because we are a close family, and I miss our get-togethers terribly. It's hardest on our youngest, I think. Aside from the fact that he has no grandparents, he doesn't see his extended family as often as I would like.

The other kids in our family have all been surrounded by love, not just from their parents but from their aunts, uncles, cousins and grandparents. We would get together every weekend, big gatherings full of the hustle and bustle of a large, loving family. There was always a lap to sit on, a captive audience to watch hastily devised shows, laughter and love. Those days were wonderful. It's funny, but I always picture them warm and sunny, maybe because that's how they made me feel.

Now, the thought of a family get-together is fraught with concern. Will our oldest be able to cope with it? How long will he be able to stay? What about eating? I need to make sure I'm next to him at the table, and I don't want meat carved at the table because the knife will trigger a panic attack. Does everyone remember not to expect hugs and kisses? Is there a quiet place he can go to if he's feeling anxious? Shall we take two cars so that I can bring him home if he's not coping, and you can stay with the youngest so he doesn't miss out? Plans, questions, worries…it's not as simple as it used to be.

Even when we've thought all of that through, most of the time, those gatherings still don't happen. It's hardest for our youngest son; OCD has dominated our lives since he was born. For him, there are no late nights watching the grown-ups in his family do Karaoke, or play darts, laughing our heads off and telling the same stories over and over again. There are no sleep-overs, being allowed sweets at nine at night, no secrets kept from mummy by an indulgent nan. No feeling of being part of a huge ball of love, the security and comfort that brings. That's not just OCD's fault, of course, his grandparents passing away is to blame for a lot of it, but OCD has made it hard to create a different kind of family, one that didn't include grandparents but still has everyone else. OCD has prevented us from being part of any kind of hustle or bustle, and, no matter how often our youngest son goes to see his family with just me, or his dad, it's not the same as us all being together, seeing his brother joining in and us all relaxing in each other's company.

He's very self-sufficient in many ways, our youngest son. I suppose he's used to being part of a more insular family. It breaks my heart to think of what he's missed out on. He's such a character, funny and extrovert, our youngest son would have loved all of the attention.

That's the thing, people don't realise the impact OCD has on everyone around the sufferer. The restrictions and stress robs lifestyles, changes families and pushes people into isolation. Our sisters and their families also miss the way things used to be. They're missing out on my children; my nieces and nephews miss out on time with their aunt, uncle and cousins; we're missing out on our nieces and nephews. So much changes.

I'm lucky that my relationships with my sister's three children, who are all grown up now, were formed before all this happened. We're very close and they know they can come to me for anything. I dote on them, and miss seeing them deeply. I'm so proud of them all, they're going off into the world but I'm not playing the role that I expected to. My eldest nephew moved away three years ago and I have never been to his new home. If you'd told me that would happen ten years ago, I'd have told you you were mad. There was no way I could imagine not seeing his home. Yet, here we are.

OCD changes everything. It's changed our entire family, how we interact with each other, how we socialise, how well we know each other. I miss them. I miss the easy way we would be together. I miss life without anxiety. In my head, I'm calling OCD some very unladylike names. Damn thing.

So, here's what I do. Our eldest son has many reasons why attending a family get-together is hard for him. We eat, so it's hard for him to do his rituals around that, he worries about offending them, or doing something inappropriate and he worries about any germs they may have that might make him ill. So, to help him, we set a goal. It may be a really small one like: we'll go and stay for one hour. Or, we'll go and he can eat his food separately. But, the key is, we go. Then, when we leave, we can all applaud him, because he achieved what he set out to do. A whole day may be daunting, so break it down into smaller goals with your child, ask them what they feel they would be able to do.

Of course, he doesn't always achieve his goals, often it's just too much. But, we try, and if OCD wins that battle, we go again.

TIPS

* ★ If at all possible, don't let OCD stop you from being around your extended family.

* ★ Give your child a chance to beat OCD by setting reasonable goals, like staying for a shorter duration, or sitting at the dinner table. If they do it, it's a victory so celebrate.

* ★ Educate your family and friends. The bigger the team in your child's corner, the better.

* ★ Go alone if it comes to it. You need your family. Reach out for their love and support.

* ★ It's OK to be angry if you miss a family occasion. Remember it's OCD, not your child, that's the problem.

That shape in the bed? That's your partner

Anyone that's ever had a demanding toddler will know the kind of strain those demands can put on a relationship. Suddenly, it's not about the two of you, it's not about you at all, it's all about this little person who needs so much and has to come first. Having a young person in your home with OCD can be like having a toddler again, except there's no end in sight, and you can't easily palm them off with a babysitter for an evening to unwind. The constant anxiety and fear of the future takes its toll.

Inevitably, the majority of the involvement with the condition, the treatment and management, falls to one parent. One of you needs to go out to earn a living, don't you? So, the one left behind to be the carer is often more knowledgeable and more aware of the depth of the problem. The one that's going out to work only sees snapshots of the situation. No matter how much detail you go into, they can really only see the problems from one row back, leaving you alone in the front row.

Your lives become very different, and that can be a problem. From the view of the carer, life can become extremely boring, peppered with moments of extreme stress, then back to boring again. If you worked before it all began, then you can lose your sense of identity and your confidence. It's lonely and isolating. From the view of the one going out to work every day, the contrast between your two lives can make for very difficult adjustments. They go into work and everyone's the same, chats at the coffee machine, talking about the latest TV show or sport result. The world of OCD gets left behind, until they have to go back there at the end of the day and face it all. The people at their work often don't have all the problems that they have at home, or at least they don't seem to, and that can lead to feelings of envy and frustration.

For us, we've had our sticky patches. There have been periods of time where we spoke very little. I didn't want to talk about my day, I just wanted to forget it, and he didn't want to hear it. He took refuge in his work, almost seeing it as preferable. Mind you, I don't blame him, I'd love to escape too! But, for me, that was very hard to deal with. I knew that I had nothing to talk about, I felt boring and undesirable, I couldn't imagine how I could compete with the people at his work, with their uncomplicated lives and, yes, I resented him for having that escape. I was jealous that he had somewhere to go to get away from all of this and my insecurities made me feel that there was no way he would possibly want to come back here at night. I was sure that, given the choice, he'd prefer to be with them.

There was a short period of time when even he felt that. He would look at other people's lives and yearn to be like them. He began to question our compatibility, and just wanted to be happy. We weren't getting along and I know that I was being particularly difficult. Just as our son takes his anger out on me, I took it out on him. I became someone who didn't bother with make-up, put on a lot of weight and most of our communications were resentful point scoring as I resented his lack of insight into what my day was like, and he resented my inability to be happy.

Not wearing make-up and putting on weight weren't the reason he wasn't happy, by the way, he's not that shallow, but they were symptoms of how I had changed, how I was giving up and not really caring about myself anymore. I was angry that he couldn't fix it, and he was angry about that, too.

We were like two caged animals, claustrophobic and stressed. Even the simplest of things that other families take for granted like a day out or a lazy day indoors involved stress and anxiety; there was no respite for us. Getting a babysitter and going out was difficult so we didn't do it, although I know we could've done that more and I was just using it as an excuse to wallow in my gloom, and maybe punish him a little, too.

He began to go out more on his own. With my blessing, I must add, I've never believed that there was any point to us both being stuck in, but he took the opportunity more and more often. So, I became more and more resentful, even though I'd agreed to it.

We fell into the trap of asking the same questions at the same times every day, giving the same answers and then...silence.

We'd speak about the weather, enquire about each other's day, give basic answers and move apart. We shared nothing except for our children and a house. It was a black time. The more distant he became, the more I hated him during that time. I thought, 'I have to deal with this, why should you get away with it? Why are your feelings more important than mine? I'm the one stuck here, my whole life has turned upside down, yours is only slightly affected, how dare you only think of yourself?' And he was thinking, 'None of this is my fault, I have to earn a living, I didn't ask to be in this situation, why can't you make the best of it? Why can't you think about our happiness for a change and think about what we have, rather than what you've lost?' We were both right. We were both wrong.

It couldn't continue like this and it came to a head one night with an awful conversation about our future, where we were both brutally honest with each other about how we felt. That night, the conversation was painful beyond any words I can think of to describe it to you but, in hindsight, it was the best thing that could have happened.

We were both depressed, but were handling it in different ways. Men often deal with depression less expressively; it's harder to spot. For him, he wanted to run away; for me, I wanted to go to bed, pull the covers over my head and stay there.

We could easily have gone our separate ways at that point, and a lot do. What made the difference for us wasn't anything positive, it was the simple fact that we couldn't burden our son with a family split, as he was scheduled to be admitted to hospital during the next few weeks. We resolved to do nothing until we'd got him through that, and see where we were at the end of it. Such shocking revelations on both sides did wake us up, though. Gradually, we began to be a bit nicer to each other. We made more effort to listen to each other, and tried to do things that the other one would like. It was as if, now that the pressure of saving our relationship had gone, our natural good manners took over and we were able to treat each other the way we treat other people, with respect and goodwill.

Funnily enough, what really saved us was TV! Yes, I know, TV is bad for relationships, we keep being told that, but we started to watch a particular show together – *Breaking Bad* (the one about the drug-dealing chemistry teacher) and we had something to share. We looked forward to that night, made an occasion of it. We connected over that TV in a way we hadn't connected over anything in a very long time, and it felt good. Suddenly, we were seeing each other in a different light. Instead of the man who just wanted to get away, I saw a man rushing to come home. Instead of the woman who wasn't interested in anything, he saw a woman who had opinions and spark. Those feelings spread into other areas; if we liked the same show, then we could like the same music and if we liked the same music, we had lots in common.

A relationship was built, and we became a team again. One that had been through darkness and now really appreciated each other. It's stronger, I feel it's more dependable. It's not perfect, what is? But, we know how we can be, and we understand that, beneath it all, we'll always have a drug-dealing teacher and his wayward pupil to fall back on. Thank God for Walter White.

As I started to connect with my partner, I felt myself connect with the world again. That's when I started getting back in touch with friends, forcing myself out of the black hole I'd allowed myself to fall into. I began to remember who I was, not just a mother of a child with OCD, but a woman. It feels good to know that, although I do still need reminding from time to time!

Unfortunately, from what I've heard, our experience isn't uncommon. Relationships fail under this kind of pressure. Resentments build and ultimately, the relationship ends. My advice is: try to remember who you are with and why. Set aside the resentments, they aren't really anything to do with each other, and spend some time together doing something you both enjoy. Even if you can't go out, do something indoors.

Also, and this is the part that made the biggest difference to me, only you can make yourself happy. Forget about making each other happy and make yourself happy. You'll never be happy together until you're a happy individual, so deal with whatever's making you miserable. Take responsibility for yourself; only you can do that. If you're struggling, get help. Whatever happens in your relationship will be made easier if you're stronger, so focus on you. Do the things you used to do before all the OCD and stress. Take bubble baths, get your hair done, see your friends. Watch a TV show.

It's worked for us, and I really hope it works for you, too. Even if you're not experiencing any problems, your relationship will still benefit from a little attention on yourselves.

TIPS

* ☆ Don't lose yourself in OCD.

* ☆ If you're feeling low, speak to your doctor. Don't struggle on alone.

* ☆ Be nice to each other.

* ☆ Do things that make you happy – even simple things make a difference.

★ Remember that stress shows itself in many ways. Give each other a break.

★ Talk to each other honestly, the way you used to.

★ Remember that these things too shall pass. The only thing that ever stays the same is that everything will change.

CHAPTER 9

Things I've Learned to Help Me Cope

I'm no angel. There's no halo above my head, or benevolent smile. It's always bothered me that so much of the advice I've read tells me to stay calm, step away, count to ten...etc. I'm not always very good at that, and it makes me feel like a failure when I just feel angry and frustrated. When I act like an actual human being rather than a Disney character. I can't suddenly become someone I'm not.

One thing I've learned is the absolutely huge power of laughter. When things get really bad, when our son's extremely anxious, or I'm feeling frustrated, I've found that cracking a joke works wonders. Take when our son's anxious. We've been told over and over again that he should breathe deeply, focus on his breathing, imagine a beach with gentle waves lapping on the shore, warm sun on his skin...you know the kind of thing. I'm sure that works for some people; it must because we've been advised to do it by so many professionals that I have come to believe it may just be us but...we really don't find it very helpful.

First of all, our son's OCD makes his brain very busy. His intrusive thoughts don't give him a minute's peace so he tells me that, when he imagines a beach, a sewerage pipe may pop in uninvited, pumping disgusting stuff all over the white sand! Gentle lapping waves are seething with deadly jellyfish...the warm sun is giving him cancer...no, he hasn't found that technique especially calming!

I've also tried it, to help me relax. There must be something in our family's genetics that makes it impossible, but I just can't switch my brain off! I don't have disturbing or intrusive thoughts, but I can't stop thinking! I imagine a beautiful beach, and this happens in my brain: 'This beach is lovely...should I go scuba diving or just lie in the sun. Is the water warm? I bet it is. Where is this beach? Am I in the Caribbean? I've always wanted to go to the Caribbean I wonder which island it is, St Kitts and Nevis has always appealed, that sprinter from the Olympics is from there...what was his name again...can't remember...that reminds me...the youngest needs new PE trainers...no, stop it...gentle waves...water lapping on the shore...I need a wee...' It's hopeless!

As I said, I'm sure it helps some people, and you should give it a go. I hope you'll be one of the ones that finds it relaxing, but if you're anything like me... It has been good for a laugh, though. We find it very amusing that our brains play these tricks on us, and I think it's really healthy that our eldest son he doesn't take it too seriously. There isn't any difference between what my brain does and what his does, except the actual thoughts themselves. His are distressing, mine are mundane, but our brains like to think, and that's normal. Everyone's brain likes to think. It's what it's designed to do. Any Buddhist will tell you that meditation doesn't come easily, clearing your mind takes a lot of practice, you have to work at it.

I prefer to laugh at myself, to be honest. Laughter works very well to break through anxiety as well. When our son's having a strong panic attack, no amount of logical reasoning will penetrate the anxiety – OCD has a hold on him and it doesn't let go easy. At times like these, I will often do something unexpected to make him laugh. It has to be something a bit crazy, or shocking, but, boy, it has worked wonders.

Take the time when I was lying on his bed as he paced back and forth, extremely anxious. I pretended to get an extreme itch on my leg, rolled to try and itch it, threw myself off the bed and rolled across the floor, ending upside down against the wall. He was so surprised, and it looked so ridiculous that it broke through his panic, he had to laugh. His brain shifted from his obsession to me, and I had him back enough to begin calming him down.

I've also danced the hula to Blondie, pretended to be Jane Mansfield, done a (frankly awful) impression of Marilyn Monroe singing 'Happy Birthday', pretended to see a spider and screamed at the top of my voice only to discover it was some fluff…and so much more that I can't remember. It happens all the time.

Also, his rituals can be very funny. Does that make me a bad person that I have to laugh at him sometimes? Don't get me wrong, most of the time it's really not funny, but just sometimes…it's so bizarre it's hilarious! The atmosphere can be so oppressive, so stressful, you've got to do something to break the tension, haven't you?

It's like one of my favourite movies of all time, *Steel Magnolias*. There's a scene (I won't give too much away in case you haven't seen it, and if you haven't, you really must) where the emotion is overwhelming, everyone's crying, it's very dramatic. Suddenly the brilliant Olympia Dukakis suggests that it would be a great idea to punch the equally brilliant Shirley MacLaine. Everyone is so shocked, it is so unexpected and inappropriate that they all start to laugh. Then they take a breath. Then they carry on coping. It's a brilliant example of how laughter can sometimes be the best answer. I don't know if the therapists would necessarily recommend it, but I would.

Of course, you have to really know the person you're laughing with in that kind of situation or you could make it worse. Don't go making fun of someone before you understand them whatever you do! But, when you're close, you can often get away with a lot.

It helps me just as much as it helps him. Having a good laugh is a great release. Scientifically, I've read that you release endorphins, the body's natural feel-good chemicals, when you laugh. Endorphins can create a sense of well-being and can even help temporarily reduce pain. A report published in 2011 by the University of Oxford proved that a good belly laugh helped the volunteers withstand 10 per cent more pain than those volunteers who hadn't recently had a laugh.[2] They found that the type of laughter was important, a little giggle or chuckle didn't do the trick, it had to be big, stop-it-hurts laughter. They explain that doing this makes your brain think the stomach muscle pain you get from laughing really hard is actual pain, so it releases the endorphins to help make it better. Hey presto! Instant feel-good fix!

I didn't know any of this until I sat down to write this book, I just knew what worked for us. I know that it creates distance between us and the problem; it helps regain a healthy

---

2   Dubar, R.I.M., Baron, R., Frangon, A., Pearce, E., van Leeuwin, E. *et al.* (2011) 'Social Laughter is correlated with an elevated pain threshold.' *Proceedings of The Royal Society of Biological Sciences.* Doi: 10.1098/rspb. 2011.1373. Available at rspb.royalsocietypublishing.org, accessed 13, August 2014.

perspective. Nothing seems scary when you see the funny side of it; it's not as overwhelming.

I also know that it keeps the bond between us strong. When we laugh together, he really looks at me, his body relaxes, he connects with me and we're in it together again. We're a team, him and I, and OCD is on the outside.

It helps that we both have the same daft sense of humour. Both prone to the dramatic, we can make most things funny when we put our minds to it. To an outsider, it may seem unfeeling that I laugh as much as I do. I have to say, there are times when I wonder if I should be laughing. I certainly wouldn't want anyone to get the impression that I don't care, or don't take all of this seriously. My ability to see the funny side of things may well be slightly warped at times, but it's my coping mechanism. When our son is very anxious, he will often rain spite down on me, saying things just to hurt me because I'm making him deal with something that scares him, and he gets very angry with me about it. I understand that. I wish I could just smooth things over and make it all better but I can't. Understanding where he's coming from is one thing, not reacting to it is quite another, though, and I try my hardest not to rise to the provocation, not always successfully as I've already told you. So, the thing that distances me from my own emotional reaction in these circumstances is laughter. I have to laugh, or I'll cry. Our son sees me laughing and, I hope, takes that as a sign that he hasn't caused any lasting damage, that I do understand and am not taking it personally. It helps him see me as strong enough to take it, because if I can't take it, who will? He has to be able to vent this anger on someone. What he's dealing with is so difficult, if he can't take it out on me, then I'm a poor excuse of a mother, in my mind.

So, I laugh it off. I smile at him when he's shouting at me. I show him that I'm here, that he won't ever be able to push me away, and there's nothing he could do or say that would make me love him less.

Now, that's when he's aiming it at me, not when he's talking about himself – that's an important distinction to make. I never laugh at how he feels, only at what he says sometimes, because I know that what he says isn't his actual feelings, it's just understandable anger at the situation turned into a pretty effective weapon. We've all done it.

Him seeing me laugh, or me making him laugh gives him the reassurance that he needs that I'm OK, without me having to reassure him. If I'm laughing, he isn't ruining my life, in other words. He worries about that a lot. He's not oblivious to the effect his condition has on our lives and he experiences an awful lot of guilt about it. Not that he should, it's not his fault, but he does. So, if you've got a funny bone, use it, it's been our biggest weapon, and saved us time and again.

Another thing that has proved to be invaluable is the love and support of my friends. My mates are brilliant. Do you know the most brilliant thing about them? We don't talk about OCD much. I know if it's bad and I need to talk, they'll always be there, but most of them have known me since I was about 17 and they still see me as that person. They don't just see me as a mother of a child who has OCD, they see me – Claire – the individual. They remember my sense of humour, they don't feel sorry for me, they're not overly sympathetic… they just treat me the same way as they always have, and that means I can be myself around them.

It has been critical at times to talk about something, anything, other than OCD. They help me (without really knowing it) to remember who I am, so I don't get lost in this. Having that sanctuary, an unspoiled place where OCD doesn't dominate, where I am still myself, that's priceless. I don't always want to talk about OCD, or how my day's been, or the fact that I've been up until the early hours trying to calm my son down. I don't want to explain how I feel, I want to be distracted. I want to be normal, and they give me that. A slice of normal, perfectly preserved. They would probably tell you that they don't do anything and wish they could do more. I know they do, but what they give me props me up in ways they can't imagine. If it wasn't for them, I'd be totally isolated. My life would be utterly ruled by OCD and I'd be swallowed whole by it.

For a long time, I actually allowed myself to become isolated. It was a very black place, hopeless and heavy with a physical presence that weighed me down dramatically. I didn't admit to it. I pride myself on being tough and strong, and asking for help when my son was the one who was ill seemed like a terribly selfish thing to do. I couldn't see how to hold a conversation: what would I talk about? Who would be interested in my life? One of the first things people ask you when they meet you is, 'What do you do?' I just didn't want to tell them, didn't want to say, 'I look after my son.' Maybe it was arrogant of me to think that I should be doing more, that looking after my son was, in some way, unimportant. Then I would feel guilty about that and it made things worse. If I told them I look after my son, and then admitted that he was getting worse...what did that say about my ability as a mother? I was with him every day, I spent all my time with him, and I couldn't help him. I was terrified of being judged as a failure, and even more so of being thought of as not coping.

People understand when your child has a physical illness. They know that there's precious little you can do about that other than follow doctors' advice. It's acceptable that sometimes treatments don't work and you are considered unlucky when that happens. I've found, with mental illnesses, some people react slightly differently. They try to see it as a 'proper' illness, but in the back of their minds, they still feel as if either the person suffering should snap out of it, or the person caring for them is in some way responsible. Especially the parents. We know that bad parenting can affect mental health, of course it can. Mental illness like this is different but people do still instinctively look for a cause, and trace it back to experiences. That really terrifies me. An awful whisper of 'What if that's true?' lingers in the back of my mind.

My friends are the ones who make it possible to ignore that whisper, and to find the energy to do another day. And then, there is my family. Especially my lovely sister who listens to me rant and rave, who never judges me and who knows me so well that often I don't even have to explain. She's always there to pick me up, to tell me I'm doing great when I feel like a failure and to generally be in my corner, no matter what, no matter how. These things are priceless.

It's never been my natural instinct to talk my problems through with people. I've always been a 'coper'. Letting people in to see how I really feel hasn't come easily but it has been worth the effort. Admitting that I'm having a hard time didn't make people feel I was failing as I feared it would, it made people rally around me and give me something to lean on. That's been a bit of a revelation to me. It's amazing to see how much I mean to those around me, and I don't regret giving them the chance to see what's behind the tough exterior one bit. How much more open I've become as a person since going through all of this makes me realise how closed I was before. I mean, the very idea of writing a book with actual feelings in it, my feelings no less, would have been impossible a few years ago. There was no way I'd ever have allowed anyone to realise that I wasn't as strong, as confident, as invulnerable as I pretended to be. Well, now you know!

I see now that real strength lies in taking the risk of weakness – trusting that I am strong enough to cope with expressing pain. Allowing myself to feel pain is the ultimate bravery. As has become a common statement in our house: courage isn't about being unafraid, it's about being afraid but doing it anyway.

Your OCD community

While it is brilliant to have an OCD-free zone with friends where you can put all of that to one side and just be yourself, it's also extremely helpful to connect with other parents who are experiencing the same problems as you. Knowing I'm not alone has been such a relief. Most countries have OCD groups that meet but, if your area doesn't, maybe you should consider starting one. OCD is such a common problem, I bet you'd find it'd be really popular.

Sharing your experiences, like I'm doing with you in this book, is kind of liberating. OCD loves secrets and shame, so coming out and telling it like it is feels like defying OCD, and that feels good. Also, you may make a difference to someone who is struggling and that's got to be worth while, hasn't it?

You'll be able to find your local OCD group online or at your local library, there is also an OCD resources and websites section at the end of the book. I have to say, I think there is a huge need for more general support and assistance in Canada and Australia, especially when you consider the statistic published by Sane Australia that 3 in every 100 Australians will develop OCD during their lifetime – that's about 450,000 people! Canada haven't made OCD specific statistics available, they go by the USA stats of 1 in 100, which is an awful lot of people that could really use some support. Perhaps you could be the one to set up an OCD specific charity?

Reach out, as they say. You'll be stronger for it and that will help your child in a very real way.

Hobbies

I know it sounds really obvious to say but doing something you enjoy from time to time feels like a holiday. I've always enjoyed writing so I wrote this book. I've also taken up baking, to varying degrees of success I must admit – why can't I get a cake right? I so want to be the kind of mother that has her children sniffing the air expectantly when they walk in the door, full of excitement at what treat their mum's got waiting for them. Not in our house, unfortunately. The air is sniffed, but more from a sense of trepidation than expectation. My scrambled egg cupcakes are yet to be lived down.

It's been good trying, though. It's given me something to think about, to read about, to focus on and I've enjoyed the process, even if it didn't give me the results I was hoping for. Never mind.

Find something new to do, it keeps your brain active and distracted. If you can find something you're good at, so much the better, but don't take it too seriously, you've got enough stress on your plate.

Believe it

For a while, my partner and I stopped talking about the future. It seemed pretty pointless to be making plans, dreaming about holidays when, at that time, it all felt impossible. That made us both feel quite depressed, the thought that we were stuck like this forever and had nothing to look forward to. Nowadays, we do dream. We believe, no matter what, that things will get better. That life will improve and we can achieve the dreams we wish for. We're quite optimistic, even though it can require quite a lot of effort at times. We focus on the positive with a grim determination. It's hard work, and takes a lot of energy; we aren't always able to do it but, usually, when one of us feels pessimistic, the other one is able to be the optimist and we talk each other round. Often, it's a real tag team effort from one day to the next but we get each other through it.

Being convinced that the future will be different keeps me motivated to fight OCD. We know where we want our lives to go, so OCD had better step out of our way.

TIPS

* Use humour to break the panic cycle whenever appropriate. It's OK to laugh.

* Allow your friends and family to help you. Talk to them. Be open.

* Stay focused on your future goals as a person, as a couple and as a family.

* Don't stop doing the things you enjoy. If you have to, then find other things that you enjoy to do instead.

* Reach out to your local OCD group. If there isn't one where you live, start one.

* Whatever gets you through is OK. For some it may be laughter, for others a good cry. We're all different.

CHAPTER 10

Common and Not So Common Obsessions and Compulsions

Everyone's OCD is different. No two children will be the same so it's important to trust your parental instincts on how your child responds and modify your approach accordingly. That said, there are the usual, and not so usual, suspects that a lot of children will suffer with and our son has suffered from most of them. So, I thought it might be helpful if I listed our son's obsessions and compulsions, the rituals he developed around them and the ways I found best to deal with them. It's important to remember that avoiding things because OCD makes you anxious is a ritual. Rituals aren't just things you do because of OCD, they are also the things you don't do because of OCD.

Germs/contamination

Well, this could be a chapter all on its own! To an OCD sufferer, they're everywhere, in everything. So many OCD sufferers are worried about germs, and the ways in which they protect themselves vary dramatically, which means the rituals they perform could be anything!

Our son describes his 'germy times' (the times when his germ fears are at their strongest) quite graphically. He feels he can actually see the germs on his skin, crawling over surfaces, leaving trails of bacteria that are potential killers. He imagines them burrowing into his flesh, sees vapor trails of them as he breathes in. For our son, the worst that could happen is that he could vomit. He is more afraid of germs killing us than killing him; for him, vomiting is the ultimate terror. Even though he accepts that vomiting actually purges your system of germs, that it's your body's way of getting rid of them, it's the sense of not knowing when it might happen, and not being able to stop it if it did happen, that terrifies him.

So, to avoid germs and vomiting, he will perform the following rituals.

Hand washing

This is the most commonly discussed and well known OCD compulsion. Not all children who have OCD will have this concern, but an awful lot do. Funnily enough, given the severity of our son's OCD, and his fear of germs, hand washing has been there, but is one of his compulsions that has never blown up into a huge problem.

A child who is worried about germs often obsesses about how clean their hands are. It's not helped by the amount of publicity that frequent hand washing preventing the spread of illnesses gets in the press and on TV. My pet hate is the 'touchless soap dispenser'. You just have to hold your hand under it to get a squirt of soap. The advertising campaign suggests that you wouldn't want to touch a nasty, germ-riddled soap dispenser that people have touched prior to washing their hands, so you should use a touch-free one.

Even my partner thought this was a good idea, until I pointed out that, after you've touched the dirty dispenser, what's the first thing you do? Wash your hands. That's why you've touched it in the first place. So, any germs you do come into contact with are washed off immediately. It's crazy. Then, there's the other advert where people are opening doors with their feet because they've only just washed their hands and don't want to contaminate themselves again, so you should use this new amazing soap that continues to kill germs for hours after you've washed your hands.

When did we decide that we are not safe unless we live in sterile, operating theatre conditions? Coming into contact with small amounts of germs is a good thing; if it wasn't we wouldn't have vaccines for serious illnesses, which are, after all, small amounts of the diseases themselves. It boosts our immune systems and protects us from repeated infections. A cold isn't the end of the world, nor is a stomach bug. By all means, try to avoid them, no one wants them, but, seriously, opening doors with your feet? Please.

TIPS

★ Do not buy products that exaggerate the risks of germs.

★ Be seen by your child to allow yourself to get dirty.

★ Do not substitute hand washing with using hand gels. It is still washing their hands, albeit in a different way. They have to learn to deal with 'dirty hands'.

★   If your child gets anxious about their hands being dirty, laugh it off. Never show any concern about it, no matter how anxious your child is.

★   If your child is anxious and wants to wash their hands, distract them if you can. Anything will do. You may have to resort to extreme measures to make them laugh. Make it surprising as this will break through the panic.

★   Educate yourself and your child about the benefits of germs.

★   Adopt a relaxed approach to colds and stomach bugs. When your child is afraid of germs, the best thing that could happen is for them to catch one. They're nasty, but they're over with quickly, not the end of the world. Your attitude is key.

★   Start making a note each time your child washes their hands. This will give you an average amount of times per day they're doing it and you may see a pattern of triggers that drives them to the sink.

★   Once you have an idea of how often and when the hand washing is taking place, work with your child to reduce it. It may be that a time is picked, for example, not washing their hands after touching a particular thing, or it may just be an amount, like reducing the frequency by a couple of washes per day.

★   It is vital that your child agrees with this and understands why they need to do it. It will cause more anxiety at first which will be very difficult to endure, so their determination and will to succeed is critical.

★   Discuss all your plans with your therapist first.

Avoiding food

Once an OCD sufferer gets the idea in their head that food may be contaminated, it can become a serious problem. Our son's OCD decided that white meat and dairy would make him vomit, since they are more likely to be off and white meat has to be thoroughly cooked. So he won't eat it. OCD is not content with that, though, oh no, then it moved on to all food, even water. It got to the point where he was living on fruit sweets.

If he does eat chicken or have milk on cereal, for example (the only time he will have milk), there are rituals to perform to prevent them being off, and to ensure he won't vomit. He will put cereal in the bowl, take it out of the bowl, put in, take out, put in…over and over again until it feels 'right'. Then, he checks the sell by date on the milk – anything less than three days and there's no way. Provided all this has gone well (and it's not actually lunchtime by the time he's finished), he will eat the cereal, lifting it up with the spoon, draining all the milk off back into the bowl…and then leaving over half at best. With chicken, he will check the sell by date, then check each morsel for pinkness as he goes along. It has to be breast meat since that's the whitest and it can't have sauce; he can't see if it's cooked if it has a sauce. In fact, with all food he will check the sell by date.

Eating around other people is problematic, he feels their 'germs' are in the air as they chew, and will contaminate his food. Raw food is OK: things like salad and fruit as they can be eaten raw and don't go off. With water, well, that was a little bit my fault, I'm afraid. It's so easy to say the wrong thing at the wrong time, and I just didn't think.

I was watching *Erin Brockovich* and he came into the room, asked me what it was about and I told him. Stupid. Of course, the film is about the true story of water containing poison that gave people cancer. I could honestly have kicked myself around the room as his horror-filled face looked at me and he asked if it was really a true story. Now, I could have lied and said no, that it never happened and never could. But that would just be playing OCD's game so I told him the truth. It's so hard to know what to do in those situations but I truly believe that he has to learn to deal with reality; avoiding things that make him anxious only fuels the fire.

So, he stopped drinking. Fortunately, he's over that now. It still creeps in from time to time, but he is able to process that it's OCD and understands that he has to drink or he really will get ill.

I've heard that some OCD sufferers will only eat with certain cutlery, or in a certain place in a certain way. Anything is possible and you really should be extra vigilant if OCD is trying to control or interfere with food and drink.

For our son, his weight became dangerously low so I had to think of ways to up his calorie intake within the limits OCD was placing on him. I read everything I could get my hands on about making food have more calorific value, because I wanted each bite to count. So, if he would only eat four forkfuls of mashed potatoes, I wanted those four forkfuls to have as many calories in them as possible to compensate.

Double cream became my friend. I added it to everything I could. If the recipe called for milk, I used cream. It raises the calories without raising the amount of food, so it was a good thing. Not easy for me, though, oh, how I wanted to eat my way through a plate of buttery, creamy mashed potatoes! Drooling while I cooked became a large feature of my life and, while his weight remained stubbornly low, mine happily sailed higher and higher! I also made sure I always had snacks that he liked in the house, so if he fancied a cake or something small, it was there for him.

It's easy really, just read a book about losing weight and do the opposite! Oh, how cruel for a woman who gains weight just walking past a bakery.

The main things to consider are, is your child getting the correct amount of calories per day? Boys need a few more than girls, and their age is a factor, but your doctor will be able to tell you what your child should be having. With a growing child, calcium is vital for their bone development and Vitamin D is needed to absorb calcium, so speak to your doctor if you're not sure what foods contain these things.

Proper hydration is also crucial. Again, your doctor will advise you if you're worried about the amount of fluid your child is drinking. The common signs of dehydration are dizziness, dry eyes, lips or mouth, headaches, tiredness, passing small amounts of urine less than three or four times per day and dark-coloured urine. If you notice any of these things, talk to your doctor. If you think your child isn't drinking enough, talk to your doctor. If you don't know how much they should be drinking, talk to your doctor.

Physical health comes first.

TIPS

* Never check sell by dates for your child.

* Never enter into any of the rituals surrounding food with your child.

* Wherever possible, feed your child the same as the rest of the family.

★ If your child seeks reassurance that the food isn't 'dirty' or 'off' – reassure once only. If they ask again, tell them you've already answered that question.

★ Make sure you tell your therapist immediately if your child's OCD is interfering with eating and/or drinking.

★ Consider a vitamin supplement.

★ If the range of foods your child will eat is narrow, or if the portions are small, get creative. Make sure each bite packs a calorific punch.

★ Consider seeing a dietician to get advice.

★ If you're worried about food or fluid intake, write down the times and amounts your child eats to help you build up a picture of an average day. Sometimes children are naturally slim even though they are taking enough calories, so writing it down can help you figure out what's going on. It will also help a dietician help you modify their diet.

Avoiding people

You see, anyone could have a bug that will only become symptomatic later. So, anyone is a risk. Everyone is a risk. As our son's germ fears increased, the amount of time he would spend with people decreased. He became withdrawn both physically and, as a consequence of his anxieties, mentally as well. He stopped going to school, seeing friends, family. He stopped giving hugs and kisses. He even stopped sitting on chairs others had sat on, in case they had left germs behind.

It was difficult because we still wanted to see people but it became pointless as we would just be spending our time dealing with our son's panic. And, given everything else we were worried about with him, missing out on social occasions seemed unimportant in the great scheme of things.

I'm not sure if we got that right. In fact, I'm pretty sure that allowing him to avoid social situations made attending them harder, ultimately impossible. In our defence, we were so worried about his eating (and any exposure to 'germs' would mean he would eat less) that we had to balance the priorities. Also, I confess, it was just too exhausting. But, as is the case with all OCD symptoms, the only way to stop it is to do it. So, if your child is scared other people may make them ill, the best thing to do is to spend time with people to see what happens. It may be that they do get ill, because that happens and, if they do, they can see how they get better and that nothing OCD says needs to be listened to. So, it's still the right thing to do.

TIPS

★ Try not to allow OCD to isolate your child. Carry on seeing people.

★ If you do decide not to go to a social occasion because of OCD, ease up on yourself. Sometimes, it is just too tiring.

★ As with everything, the way to beat the anxiety is to face the anxiety.

★ Make sure you still go out even if you have to make arrangements to have someone else watch your child. It is good for you, and good for your child to see that you go out, come back, and nothing bad happens.

Avoiding touching things

To avoid contact with germs, our son, along with many OCD sufferers, is very careful about what he touches. He won't flush a toilet at home, and won't use a toilet anywhere else. He won't touch door handles, hand rails on stairs or escalators, buttons on lifts or surfaces in a restaurant. Anything that other people have touched is off limits.

Of course, he has to touch some things sometimes and, to manage this, he will only wear long-sleeved clothing, so that he can pull the sleeve down over his hand to provide a barrier between him and the germs. That's not a big deal in the great scheme of things, except when it's warm out; then it can be an issue.

If he just preferred to not use public toilets, who cares, right? I'm not massively keen on it, and most people are hygiene conscious in those situations. So, who cares if he won't touch a hand rail, or press a button in a lift?

That's the difference between somebody who doesn't like public toilets and somebody who has OCD. Our son isn't content to just not touch them, the anxiety he experiences at the thought that he might touch them, or he might be exposed to germs in another way that he won't be able to control makes him avoid the situation entirely. He can't just avoid it and do everything else. It doesn't work that way.

It does mean that, wherever we are, whatever we're doing, he isn't really properly engaged with us. He is completely preoccupied with avoiding all the things OCD tells him he should and it leads to him being very distracted, not following conversations, not relaxing or enjoying himself.

It's not the most fun in the world, trying to enjoy a family treat out to a restaurant and OCD taking over. We try to relax and enjoy but it's not always possible. There are so many things to remember, we don't even notice ourselves doing it anymore.

TIPS

★ OCD will make your child very anxious to avoid things that are 'dangerous'. Try to be patient. The anxiety isn't alleviated just by not touching them, OCD will make them worry about all the other 'dangers' that are around at the same time.

★ Make sure you touch all the things your child won't, and be seen to do so without making it a big deal.

★ Your child will only combat the anxiety by actually touching the things they are avoiding but this must be done at your child's pace. Never force your child to touch something against their will. They must decide that they are ready.

Sexual obsessions

Often, these thoughts and images are of a graphic sexual nature. Now, I imagine a lot of parents will find that very hard to deal with. Our son's thoughts are mostly about rape, sometimes of him being raped, sometimes it's one of his family being raped. They are horribly distressing. It took a long time for him to be able to talk to me about them because he felt so guilty, as if he was some kind of pervert for having these ideas in his head. He's not a pervert, of course, he just has OCD and it's important to make that very clear.

The thing to remember at all times is that the intrusive thought is not a thought they agree with. It isn't representative of their opinion in any way. What it is representative of is the opposite of their opinion. In fact, our son's intrusive thoughts about rape are a clear sign that this is the most awful, most distressingly, completely wrong thing to him. If he agreed with it, or believed it, it wouldn't make him anxious, would it? No, OCD will throw in things that are absolutely repellent to you, not things that you believe.

So, remember that if your child has sexual obsessions, they aren't your child's thoughts, or fantasies, it's OCD.

Believe me, if you ever manage to persuade your child to really tell you what they imagine in their heads, it's truly awful. Then, they will feel terrible that they had that thought, convinced that they must be evil, there must be something wrong with them that they are able to imagine such horror. OCD can even jump in there as well, and give your child the strong belief that they do actually believe it and that they are, in fact, evil. The panic you see in their eyes when they are experiencing this is enough to tell you that the absolute opposite is true.

For my son, he imagines me being raped. It's almost like a movie in his mind where he can see a man (often Charles Manson as we've already discussed), creeping into my room, or coming up behind me in the kitchen, or leaping out on me as I walk through the park. He can see me scream, he can see the knife at my throat, see the fist smash into my mouth, the blood pour out, hear me begging for mercy as my throat is cut wide open. Or, he has a female friend over and his intrusive thoughts are that he is going to touch her inappropriately, or sexually assault her and that she's not safe near him.

Other people often have a obsession that, if they touch or interact with a member of the same sex, they may be gay. Or, others might think they are because they've been unable to stop themselves giving the impression that they're gay. Often, the stress of just being around members of the same sex is so high that it's avoided altogether. It's as if, somehow, the interaction will determine their sexuality and they won't have any control over it. Some poor people also worry that they will touch a child inappropriately and avoid children at all costs, such is their distress.

Sexuality and sexual violence is a very common theme with OCD's obsessive thoughts and can manifest itself in many ways. How it does is very much to do with what the sufferer finds most distressing. Whatever that is, is exactly what OCD will tell them is going to happen. That's how it works.

Causing offence

Our son worries like crazy about offending people, especially people of a different race to us. He gets flooded by intrusive thoughts and urges that he will shout racial abuse at them, or if they are wearing clothing unique to their culture, that he will grab the clothing and try to remove it. He basically has intrusive thoughts that he is a raving racist and people of different races or religions from him are not safe to be around him.

It's laughable because, as a family, we are the most tolerant group. Racism of any kind is absolutely not a feature in our lives and is a totally unacceptable thing. You see? OCD takes what we believe would be the worst possible things, and makes us believe they are happening, or that they are possible. It's really interfered with our lives because it gives him even more reason to be afraid of the outside world. He'll avoid places where it is likely that he will be near people of different races (which is anywhere).

He also gets urges to randomly insult people. The actual insult depends upon the person; it could be anything but he worries that he will say something to offend them. This could be a person who is overweight, a disabled person, an old person, someone wearing bright clothes...anything...anyone.

The result of this bombardment of thoughts is that he is enormously anxious when he goes out; nobody's safe in his mind. OCD also tells him that he will say something offensive to the 'wrong person' one day and that person will react violently, and kill him.

Also, he will analyse any interaction with people after the fact. So, if he does see people and have a conversation, he will often spend quite a lot of time going over what he said or did, looking for ways in which he may have said something that caused offence. He will also often look for reassurance that someone isn't offended by him; that's the ritual part. 'Are you upset with me, mum?', 'No', 'Did I upset you though, mum?', 'No', 'I didn't mean to look at you funny, mum', 'You didn't', 'But, if I did, I didn't mean it', 'I'm not talking about this anymore', 'Why? See? You are upset with me aren't you?' Oh, good grief.

Again, the thing that needs to happen here is: go sit in a room filled with people, and let's see what happens. The more they do it, the quieter OCD becomes about it.

Confession

Our son recently began to feel as if he needed to confess to things he hasn't done. It hasn't become a big thing, yet, and we are trying to head it off. I've heard a few people talk about this symptom. Some poor people have this one so badly that they won't go out for fear they will go to a police station and confess to a murder, be believed and sent to jail.

I bet you know by now what I'm going to say should be done? That's right, go into a police station and see if you confess. Wait for the anxiety to go down on its own, with no rituals to help it, and prove to yourself that OCD lies.

Hurting himself or others

This is an absolutely enormous obsession for our son. He gets the urge to hurt other people, or to harm himself. Now, I say urge because that's the closest you can get to describing it, but it's more the overwhelming feeling that you are going to do something absolutely terrible and you can't stop yourself from doing it. Panic sets in because you really feel as if you're going to lose control and do it.

He'll get the urge to push me in front of a car, or grab the steering wheel as we drive, or pick up a knife and stab me, or push someone down the stairs...the list goes on. So, to be sure he won't do any of those things, he won't walk behind me, so he can't push me, he sits on his hands in the car, he won't go into a room if there's a knife in it. Avoidance is the only way he can cope with the anxiety of these thoughts and urges, they are very powerful and terrifying. That's the ritual.

Of course, what he needs to do, and what we have done, is do it anyway. We have stood with him holding a sharp knife pressed against my stomach, for as long as it took for his anxiety to come down. He shook and cried and sweated but he did not stab me. Of course he didn't, he would never hurt anybody and the only way to prove that to him is for him to be in the situation and see what happens. The same principle applies: face it.

Don't be alarmed if your child has urges to hurt others. OCD is a creature of opposites: if OCD is saying they will do something, it really means it's the last thing on earth they'd ever do. I've said it before, it's like they have a bully living inside their heads, and it will use any and all weapons at its disposal to control them. Nothing is off limits, and the more it can flood their minds with these awful images and thoughts, the more the child will be under its spell. There I go again, giving OCD a personality, but I truly feel it does. I mean, I know it's a medical condition, but it feels and behaves like a parasite inside my child's head that no one can operate on to remove. This parasite whispers to him.

He also gets the urge to hurt himself, and the worst culprit for this is the urge to jump from an open window. As a result of this, he won't enter a room above ground floor if a window's open. It's so bad he just runs. Urges to stick pins into himself, especially his eyes, cut himself with a razor, hit himself in the face with anything heavy, throw himself down the stairs, drown himself, stab himself, take an overdose, drink chemicals…you name it, he gets the urge to do it to himself. Resultingly, he has many, many avoidance rituals. Pretty much everything. It'd be easier for me to tell you what he doesn't avoid, actually.

When a child has such a distressing obsession, they will try to stop it from coming true by doing a ritual, and remember avoiding something is also a ritual. If they do, then it's the ritual that you need to target. Stop the ritual, the cycle is broken and the obsession will fade, in time.

Deadlines

Sometimes I'll walk into a room, usually the kitchen, and see our son running around like a headless chicken with his head chopped off, desperate to complete a task before 'time runs out'. Usually, if he's boiling the kettle or has something in the microwave, he 'has' to have everything ready before the kettle boils or the microwave finishes. But, and this is where OCD is really sly, he isn't 'allowed' to add more water to the kettle at the beginning to try and give himself more time. So, if there's only a little water in the kettle, he'll be flying around, getting the milk out, the cup, the teaspoon, putting the teabag and sugar in the cup, taking the lid off the milk, in about 25 seconds. Why does OCD want him to do this? Because, apparently, if he fails in this mission, I will die. Timers are a large problem, the defined amount of time gives OCD a real foothold, a measurable exercise. So, he doesn't make hot drinks…which is very upsetting because I was so looking forward to having a child old enough to keep the caffeine coming without me having to get up!

TIPS

⋆   OCD likes secrets. Your child may not tell you if they're struggling with obsessions and rituals. Watch for signs of anxiety that can't be explained.

⋆   No matter what, no matter how bizarre, how offensive, how strange – the obsessions are not your child's thoughts. They are OCD's thoughts. Remember that your child is not OCD, they are separate. When you speak to your child about it, speak to your child, not OCD.

Offending God and religious mania

Now this one, I am fascinated by. My son has this symptom and it really makes no sense. We are not practising religious types, I mean, we have our beliefs but religion doesn't play a major role in our day-to-day lives. OCD tells our son, though, that God can deliver terrible punishments if you offend him and so, he feels he can't take any chances. So, he began to make the sign of the cross. That ritual has really taken hold and he does it continuously throughout the day. He'll have an intrusive thought, and then has to make the sign of the cross until it feels 'right', until OCD says that God will forgive him. Isn't that awful? Scaring a child like that? Again, it makes me see OCD as a living, breathing thing and, boy, do I wish I could be locked in a room, just me and it, for half an hour.

I can only imagine the problems this particular obsession could cause in a family that does have strong religious beliefs. I often wonder how I would feel if I were them, if my child was worrying about something that my belief system actually preached.

Many religions do tell us that we should fear judgement and that we must live our lives according to a set of morals or even rules. How hard it must be if OCD takes that to the extreme. How do you find a balance? Find a balance you must, however. It is one thing to want to be the best person you can be, to obey the teachings of your church, quite another to allow your life to be stalled to achieve that.

For me, I suppose, I would look for signs that these thoughts are not giving my child any peace. If religious observance is causing anxiety, if your child is actually becoming more anxious worrying about teachings that you find comfort in, then OCD has gotten hold of this idea and that would be my cue to step in. Your child should understand that difference, and you, with the help of your religious leader perhaps, will be demonstrative in taking religion out of the control of OCD and giving it back to your child as the positive thing it's intended to be.

Dealing with that obsession has been tricky and we're not completely over it as yet. The same principles apply as with other obsessions, though. He needs to not make the sign of the cross, and see what happens. He will see that (i) God will not punish him and (ii) his anxiety will fade. Finding the courage to do that is really hard for him, though. Who would really want to risk the wrath of God? Even though our son knows that his rituals aren't stopping God punishing him, there is enough doubt, enough 'what if' to make him too afraid to try.

Organisation

Another very well-known symptom of OCD is the need to organise items in a particular way. This could be the tins in your kitchen cupboard, your CD collection or your bookshelf. Many people interpret this as a desire to keep things tidy, when in actual fact that isn't the case. It's true that most things need to be well organised for an OCD sufferer but their interpretation of that organisation varies widely.

Our son's OCD likes his remote controls to be lined up, biggest to smallest, on his bedside table. Very neat. It also likes his bookshelf to be organised in a way that anyone else would think is total disarray but everything has its place, and you can't move it. It drives me mad.

As always, OCD is different for everybody. Our son will visit a supermarket and spend ages organising the shelves to make them orderly, but sometimes, that order will mean that he 'has' to take a tin of hot dogs that is very tall, and place it in the middle of the baked bean tins. It's not what many people expect an OCD sufferer to do, as they expect uniformity but OCD makes it's own rules. Another OCD sufferer may come along after him, see the hot dog tin, feel that it's in the 'wrong' place and move it. It all depends on what their OCD is saying to them.

In his own room, he can do what he likes. OCD is not allowed to dictate how I organise the rest of my home, and we've had quite a few battles where I've had to defend our right to have things the way we want them, not the way OCD wants them.

The major problem with OCD wanting our son to have the items in his room in certain places is the anxiety that it causes if someone else should go into his room. Even if they are told not to touch anything, which they are, he experiences very high anxiety just in case they do. So, he spends all his time actually watching their body language for signs that they may be about to touch something they shouldn't. He isn't listening to conversation, he isn't relaxing, he is hyper-vigilant. At the first hint that they may be thinking about going near his bookshelf, he will jump up and stand in front of it to head them off. Not a great visit, or a particularly pleasant social tactic but he is lucky that his friends understand. Again, of course, the way for him to overcome this is to allow his friend to touch his bookshelf and wait to see what happens, but he's not ready for that.

One day.

TIPS

★ Do not allow OCD to change the way you organise your home. Stand your ground.

★ Understand your child's need to have things a certain way but never organise them that way yourself.

★ Do not avoid cleaning your child's room. If things are moved then they are moved. This will confirm the message you are sending that it's OK to move things, and that you don't listen to OCD.

★ Never deliberately move things without a reason, however. Your child must decide to challenge this ritual and needs to know that you can be trusted.

Perfectionism

The need for things to be 'right' is a massive player in the OCD game. It impacts on everything, from getting dressed in the morning, to school and how food is presented on a plate. Everything. For our son, it's become so bad that he finds it almost impossible to write, draw or even read.

An OCD sufferer will often struggle with finishing school work because they have to keep re-doing it until it's perfect. Sometimes the work will look perfect when they've finished and sometimes it will look a total mess with crossed-out words and repetition all over it; it depends on the child.

The feeling of it not being 'right' is described by our son as an overwhelming sense of dread. Intrusive thoughts play a large role, with OCD whispering that people will think he's stupid if it's not perfect, or laugh at him. So, he becomes more and more anxious, judging all his efforts against an impossible OCD measure of 'rightness'. When I look at what he's done, it looks fine to me. But he sees all the errors, the crosses on the Ts that aren't the same, a comma that's too long, a gap that's too big. His vision is like Spidey-sense (one of Spiderman's superpowers), with everything under a microscope, and he sees things that just aren't there.

Often a child with OCD will take forever to finish a task, but making them stop before they're finished is excruciating for them. Sometimes, you just have to stop them, though, or who knows how long they'd go on for? Could be forever! When you do have to force them to stop before they're ready, the resulting anxiety they experience can be devastating, so be prepared for that. They can't help it, OCD is usually screaming at them all the terrible things that could happen if they stop. They may be being told that you will die, they will die, you will get cancer, anything and everything is possible and usually totally illogical. Ride it out, their anxiety will pass, and when what OCD is insisting could happen, doesn't happen, I hope they will be able to put that knowledge to good use.

For our son, working on a laptop is easier; there's something about the laptop being the thing that is actually forming the words that takes the responsibility for how it looks away from him. Also, he gets more time to finish tasks if needed, within reason and, most importantly, he is not punished if tasks are not completed. As long as he gives it his best shot, that's good enough.

TIPS

★ Don't fall into the trap of reassuring your child often that the work they are doing is perfect.

★ Don't be afraid to give your child's work the same critique as you would any other child's.

★ If you have to stop your child from finishing a task before they are ready, try to find out what OCD is saying will happen. Then, when the anxiety has passed, point out that this did not happen and ask your child what they have learned from that.

★ Remind your child that their anxiety will pass.

★ Tell your child's school if their work is being affected. There may be another way of working that will help.

★ Although we should never adjust things to accommodate OCD, education is crucial so it's OK to look for reasonable alternative ways of working, such as extending homework deadlines or working on a laptop.

Good luck charms

We're all a bit superstitious. Whether it's walking under ladders, stepping on cracks in the pavement, breaking a mirror or not crossing on the stairs, most of us know these things are nonsense but we still go along with them. Then, there are common objects that a lot of us carry as good luck charms like four-leaf clovers, a rabbit's foot or something more personal to us like a particular pair of socks or piece of jewellery. We like to believe that not doing certain things, or carrying certain objects will, in some way, boost our luck, help us win the match, get the job, pass the exam etc.

OCD takes these medieval hangovers to the extreme. Often it starts the way it does for most people. Say you were a football player going into a big game, and you wear a particular pair of socks for the first time. Say you win that game. The next game, you wear your 'lucky socks' and you win again. From then on, those are your game socks, and you won't play without them. You know it's silly but...just in case...

An OCD sufferer may go to school one day, and OCD is telling them that they might be exposed to germs, and get ill. Then, as happens more often than not, they don't get ill. OCD remembers almost everything they did that day in minute detail and tells them that the only reason they didn't get ill was because of all those things they did and they must do them exactly the same way every day to protect themselves. The OCD sufferer will obey but there are so many details that they may get it wrong in parts, so have to go back and start again, or OCD may make them worry that they've got it wrong and should start again. So, they get stuck in an endless ritual, desperately trying to replicate the day when nothing bad happened, believing that it was the ritual that protected them, not just the fact that it didn't happen. The randomness of life cannot be entertained.

Often, an OCD sufferer will latch onto a particular number that is 'safe' and OCD will tell them that anything that isn't that number is, therefore, 'not safe'. So, they spend a lot of time counting things in their head, the letters on a poster, on a page, the number of people on the bus, the number of steps they are taking, anything. And they count in blocks of the 'safe' number. Or, it may be that there's a particular 'unsafe' number that the sufferer has to ensure they are not exposed to, like the number 13 for our son.

You may find strange things being kept in bags or pockets like acorns or pebbles or old food wrappers. There may even be a rhyme that is said, or a sequence of words said in the 'right' way at the 'right' time. These are all talismen, and an OCD sufferer attaches huge importance to them.

Our son has many of these talismen. There are the more understandable ones, ones that it makes sense to be attached to, such as a teddy bear, and there are the more bizarre ones such as a pair of underpants that have been shoved down the side of the bed and must be left there. Gross.

As you will by now have guessed, the way to rid your child of these dependencies is to let the talisman go, trigger the anxiety, do no rituals to manage the anxiety and wait for it go down on its own. Then, see if anything bad does happen without them.

TIPS

★ Anything can be a good luck charm, from a routine to a phrase or an object.

★ Never confiscate a good luck charm without the consent of your child.

★ Encourage your child to do an experiment to see if anything bad will happen if they don't use their good luck charm, but be patient – it may take them some time to agree to that as OCD will probably have some very dire consequences on offer. Your child has to be ready to defy OCD.

Checking

The French name for OCD used to be 'La Folie de Doute' which means 'the Doubting Disease' and that really is an appropriate title. OCD sufferers doubt everything. They doubt their belief that rituals don't work, they doubt their ability to stop themselves from hurting others, they doubt that their hands are clean, that germs won't kill them. One of the most common ways that this doubt manifests itself is in the constant checking and rechecking of things.

Usually, it's checking things that would be dangerous if they were overlooked. Checking the door is locked, the oven's off, the window's shut are all very, very common. You or I would think, 'Did I lock the back door?' and probably go to make sure. Once we'd seen that we had locked the door, we'd be satisfied. But the doubt that an OCD sufferer experiences just keeps going and they can check something hundreds of times and still not be totally convinced. OCD tells them that, if the door is unlocked, the house will be burgled and the burglars may still be there when you return home, and something terrible may happen. So they make sure. Then they make sure again. Then, they might have got it wrong, so they make sure again. Over and over.

That kind of makes sense, doesn't it? In a way. You can at least see where they're coming from.

Our son checks that his nose hasn't grown massively huge overnight.

I know, really, it's OK to laugh, I do. Who does he think he is, Pinocchio? OCD makes him doubt that his appearance will remain the same from one day to the next. That's also to do with one of OCD's nasty relatives which we'll talk about in the next chapter, but the checking is an OCD feature.

So, they can check anything, which can be really disruptive because they may keep going back inside to check, or to their room over and over again. Getting out on time is not easy! The best way I've found to deal with all the checking is to be firm about the repetition. It will feel a bit cruel to tell them that's enough, because they will probably become very anxious, but it's the kindest thing.

TIPS

* Never help check things for your child. This will only confirm that it's important.

* Limit the number of times that something can be checked and kindly, but firmly, insist that they stop when the limit is reached.

> ⋆ Do not over-reassure that whatever it is they need to check was OK. Tell them once that the door is locked, or whatever, then simply say that you've answered that question if they ask again.
>
> ⋆ If getting out of the house on time is a problem and your child is often late for school, or to lessons if they are checking during school time, make sure your school understands the challenges and knows how to deal with them.

Intrusive thoughts, images and urges

Less is spoken about this obsession. Intrusive thoughts and images are thoughts and pictures that pop into your mind without you wanting them – intruding on your mind. This is a real problem for our son; he has them all the time and they really upset him. It's hard to combat these as it's not like a physical obsession that you can address practically.

If we're honest, we all have intrusive thoughts from time to time. The most common one is when we're at a train station, and we can suddenly get an overwhelming feeling that we're going to push someone who's standing close to the edge of the platform, or maybe jump ourselves, as I've said before. It's normal.

If we think of it in terms of a phobia, one of the most common ones is a fear of heights or acrophobia. I have this, well, not exactly a proper phobia – I can go up high but I really don't like it and would prefer not to if at all possible. For me, and for many others with this fear, it's not the fear of falling that scares me, it's the feeling that I'm being somehow drawn to the edge and will jump off. I feel like I'm not going to be able to stop, as if I'm not in control. It's very OCD-like, that thinking, but is a common feature of acrophobia. So, you see, our brains all work that way sometimes – it's perfectly normal. When you have OCD, however, you can't do what the rest of us do in that situation and reason with yourself. When I have to go up high, I will expect the anxiety, remind myself that it's just a fear and I am able to manage. I don't have the need to perform a ritual to manage, I can go solo.

Intrusive thoughts can be about pretty much anything.

Insults

This is where the bully really shows its colours. Intrusive thoughts aren't always about what you may do, they can also be about who you are.

Our son suffers through endless insults, where OCD tells him that nobody likes him, that he bores me, that he's stupid, talentless, ugly, worthless. It must be absolutely exhausting. Anyone who's ever endured bullying, or has been called names, can appreciate how that makes you feel. Now, imagine that the person that made you feel that way followed you around all day and all night and never stopped putting you down so that every time you opened your mouth to speak, every time you tried to achieve anything, you were immediately told that whatever you were doing was ridiculous…do you think you'd ever get anything done?

It never fails to amaze me that OCD sufferers are able to do as much as they do, given what they are putting up with. I couldn't do it. All it takes for me to refuse to go to a party is the wrong look at my outfit! God forbid someone should actually say I don't look nice; that would be devastating and would result in a tearful refusal to go out, a few hours crying in a darkened room, and then at least a day of sulking. Our son and other OCD sufferers are told that all the time, and yet they still try to function. Their strength humbles me.

The random ones

Every day, our son has thousands of random thoughts that pop up unannounced. You can't predict them; they don't have a pattern. He'll have a thought that he 'has to' get in the door first, or last. Then, he may have a thought that he has to sit on the floor for five minutes, or bring a cup down into the kitchen, or wear a certain T-shirt. It could be anything, so often our son will do something really bizarre that makes us stop in our tracks, and usually laugh. OCD likes to keep him busy with OCD. It doesn't like him to have any room for himself in his mind and this is its way of making very sure of that.

TIPS

★ Keep communication open with your child so they can talk to you about their intrusive thoughts.

★ Get your head around talking about sexual matters, often quite unpleasant ones. Do not appear embarrassed and never ever discipline them in any way for having these thoughts. Your child has done nothing wrong; it's part of the condition and your child doesn't want to have these thoughts.

> ★ Watch for rituals after intrusive thoughts. Target the ritual associated with it, allowing the anxiety caused by the thought to come down on its own.
>
> ★ We all have intrusive thoughts from time to time. Be open about this with your child. Normalise the situation.

Other rituals

We know that avoiding things is a ritual and our son does a lot of that, and I've explained some of his other rituals, but here's a list of the things he does at various times. Some of them are done all day every day, some only once or twice a month, but I wanted to give you an idea of how different rituals can be. They're not always what you expect and they don't have a common theme for the most part. He does them mostly in response to intrusive thoughts which occur constantly for him, and it can be to prevent a loved one's death, his own death, or to protect himself from anything. So all day, all night, every day, every night, he'll be doing at least one or more of the following:

- making the sign of the cross
- hand washing
- touching wood
- sitting on hands
- biting lips/gums
- repeated blinking

- staying still
- counting
- tapping
- kneeling
- throwing head back
- gulping for breath
- repeating words/sentences
- counting possessions
- organising possessions
- checking sell by dates
- checking food is cooked
- not putting items back into the fridge
- hiding items
- stealing items
- going through the entire list of stored movies one by one before selecting the one he wishes to watch.

It's a lot, isn't it? I hope your child's list isn't as long as this, and that their rituals are less frequent, but that's how it is for our son.

CHAPTER 11

Related Conditions
Other Nasties in OCD's Gang

Did you ever notice how that bully in the playground is almost never alone? Bullies love company. They love to surround themselves with like-minded individuals who make them feel more powerful and help them control their victim. As OCD is, essentially, a big fat bully, it of course has its gang of followers that can jump in and make things even more difficult.

These conditions are considered to be 'on the OCD spectrum of disorders' and people who suffer from one of them will often find characteristics of the others involved. The most common related conditions are:

- body dysmorphic disorder (BDD)
- eating disorders
- trichotillomania
- compulsive skin picking
- Tourette syndrome
- depression.

Our son has actually experienced all of these to some degree or another, with the worst being body dysmorphic disorder and anorexia.

BDD and eating disorders

For him, the body dysmorphic disorder centres around his hair, his nose and his thighs. He constantly checks in the mirror to see if his nose is looking very big and if his hair looks OK. He'll check roughly every ten minutes or so that the gap between his thighs is still there, so he hasn't got fat. That's where it crosses over with anorexia, you see?

The anorexia began a while ago and I'm told it's not totally uncommon especially if the person with OCD is restricting food intake due to contamination fears and is underweight as a result. Our son was, of course, eating very little and is very underweight so, when he was hospitalised and realised that there was no way he was ever getting out if he didn't eat, he put a little weight on. He hated it.

It was so confusing for him. On the one hand, there were his fears about getting ill and dying and he knew that if he didn't eat properly, he would become very ill indeed. That terrified him. On the other hand, there were these awful feelings about being overweight and not wanting to get fat. He found himself not knowing who to please. Some days, his being underweight fears win and he eats; some days his being overweight fears win and he doesn't. Every day his fear of vomiting wins and he eats very little.

He's a complicated little soul.

I've found dealing with his anorexia and BDD particularly difficult. As most women will admit, I'm not entirely happy with my body. There have been times when dressing to go out, that I have been mildly hysterical, changing outfits numerous times, convinced I look terrible. Tears, and some high-pitched screeching have been known if I've gained weight and am forced to look in the mirror. Wearing a swimming costume is especially traumatic; I don't think I've ever met a woman who didn't find that made her self-conscious. Considering I've only ever met normal women, and not supermodels, I assume then that we're all the same. Men aren't immune, although they seem to be less concerned in general. We've all seen the beer belly dads strutting their stuff in too-short swimming trunks, haven't we? They seem supremely confident, they're having a great time and their appearance doesn't interfere with it at all. At least, that's how it seems on the surface – who knows what may be going on behind the scenes? But I do know some men who aren't as confident, who would love to look like a Greek god, and are painfully aware that they don't. So, having my own insecurities has made it quite hard to know how best to manage our son's. His have gone from insecurity to obsession, but the basic root of the problem is one I can really relate to. I don't like my teeth. I'm really insecure about them. When I was little, I sucked my thumb and, as a result, my upper jaw formed around my thumb so, actually, it's not my teeth that protrude, it's my jaw. Perfect, beautiful. I don't open my mouth to smile in photos, and cover my mouth when I laugh. For my sister, it's her nose – she's sure it's huge; for my best friend, it's her thighs; other friends dislike anything from their feet to their tummy. We all have something we'd like to change and it doesn't matter how many times we are told that we're crazy, and that we look great, those are our weak points.

The way most of us handle this is to be very good at disguising these imperfections: good make-up, hold-it-all-in clothing and push-up bras are all things that we girls use to improve an area and make the most of our best bits. So, having an insecurity is absolutely normal, that when we start to check during the day that those imperfections haven't changed, that they are still disguised, to the point where our day is disrupted, that's when it is turning into an obsession. It's all about how big the impact is on how we live our lives. If you hate your birthmark, but cover it with make-up then go have a good day, checking it when you use the bathroom but not going to the bathroom just to check it, then there's no problem. It's when you start visiting the bathroom, or looking in the mirror constantly, that's when it has become a disorder.

Knowing I have insecurities about appearance which are very similar to those our son has is hard, funnily enough (you would've thought it would make it easier). It's hard because I don't really know how to make yourself totally confident in your appearance. I've never achieved that for myself, so I have very few words of wisdom for our son. In this regard I have real empathy, whereas with OCD problems, I have sympathy as I don't suffer from that personally.

I am being very careful about how I discuss weight and appearance and I am trying not to moan about small imperfections anymore. I've even put a swimming costume on with a smile on my face, not looked in the mirror and skipped out the door! That, my friends, is a miracle right there. The last thing I want is for me to in any way encourage or endorse these fears, so I have to not have them, or at least be seen to not have them myself. When I do show that I wish I was taller, or more bronzed, I do it with a wry smile now, and try to show him a more positive way to manage your insecurities. I shrug and say that there are women who would love to be short like me, and we're never happy with what we've got, we always want what someone else has. I'm not sure if that's helping, but it's definitely not giving OCD any ammunition to use against him, and that's the main thing.

Trichotillomania

He went through a really worrying stage with trichotillomania. If you didn't know, that means 'pulling hair out'. For our son, he would pull hair out from his head, especially around the hairline at the front, and pubic hairs. He said he would get the feeling, or OCD would give him the feeling, that one of his hairs was 'wrong'. He could feel this individual hair and, to him, it would be really obvious, it would feel awkward and different from all the other hairs around it. So, he'd pull it out, so his hair was 'right'. Then, OCD would do it again, and again, until he had a noticeably receding hairline. I didn't inspect the pubic area, if I'm honest, as some things are a bit too personal for a child to reveal, and I allowed him some privacy but kept talking to him about the amount of hair that he was pulling. Other people might pull out eyebrow hairs, or even eyelashes. OCD will make them feel that hairs are 'wrong' and must be removed. I was ever so upset about his hairline; there was something about this visual proof that he was doing something to himself physically that was more alarming than all the other symptoms. It lasted for about six months and then, as happens so often with OCD compulsions, it faded and he moved on to something else.

Skin pricking

Skin picking is another area where he can go through very bad stages for a few weeks, and then not do it all for months. We're not sure what makes it happen, but every now and again, OCD feels that parts of his skin are 'wrong' and have to be picked off. OCD seems to have a particular problem with skin on our son's feet and this is where the majority of the skin picking happens. Because it was in an area I don't see much, it took a long time for me to realise that something was happening. In fact, it was only when he'd hurt his foot so badly, created such a deep gouge that he was limping and there was blood in his socks, that I found out. OCD had moved on to driving drawing pins into this particular spot on his foot, to remove the skin, and it got infected. So, although skin picking seems quite innocent on the surface, it can become a bit more of an issue and you should be quite vigilant about it.

Tourette Syndrome

Tourette syndrome has moved in from time to time, the urge to shout swear words. It's like an urge he gets and can't control, the swear word just comes out, which makes it even harder for him to be able to mix with others. I have to say, I can't help it, but I do find it funny. I know it's not funny and it's ever so distressing for the person suffering it, but I have had to leave the room to hide my mirth. I'm a terrible person. There was a time when I persuaded our son to go out to the park opposite on his own for a five-minute walk. I was just trying to get him out of the house, let him see he could do it, increase his confidence. But, while he was there, he shouted the 'F' word really loudly, which was heard by an elderly lady who was walking her dog, and she nearly walked into a lamp post! The image I had in my head really made me laugh, and it took a few minutes for me to compose myself enough to commiserate. The whole swearing issue should maybe bother me more, and if it weren't for the fact that it's not really him swearing, it's OCD, I would be more strict about it but, honestly, it's so out of character for him to do anything so rebellious, I find it hysterical.

As I've said about laughter before, although he's upset, seeing my reaction takes the awfulness out of it for him. For him, it's a terrible thing to do, and he imagines people being highly offended, that it makes him a really bad person. Then, he tells me and I laugh, and suddenly, the monster shrinks; he can see he's not a bad person, and he won't be in trouble. His anxiety fades, and OCD is kept firmly in the background. I am sure that, if I were to react with anger, or even concern, OCD would use that as 'evidence' that it's an awful thing to do, and he should stay in his room away from people to protect society from the monster that he has become. No way is OCD going to have that. He finds that these urges are strongest around young children, which makes sense as that would be the worst possible time to swear, so OCD will definitely latch on to that. He goes to unbelievable lengths to avoid swearing. He has bitten his tongue so deeply that he drew blood, bitten his lip so hard for so long that part of his flesh actually died from lack of circulation. Maybe I should swear more at home. Maybe that would stop OCD from holding swearing up as something you should never do and, if it weren't for the fact that I have another, younger, child, I would. It's hard to teach him that swearing is wrong when you do it yourself, though, and I do firmly believe that swearing should be kept to a minimum and there are better ways to express yourself. OCD using me against myself, that's a low blow.

Depression

As far as depression goes, I'd be more worried about him if he didn't find the situation he's in depressing, if I'm honest. His life absolutely sucks, and he gets depressed. I say, thank God for that, at least he can see that his life sucks – if he didn't, there's no way it would ever improve.

The thing is, there's feeling fed up, and actual depression. When you suffer from real, clinical depression, you believe that nothing can ever change. The world looks black to you and you have no energy or motivation to improve it. That makes therapy very tricky as, deep down inside, our son doesn't believe he deserves a happy life due to his depression. Addressing these issues will make engaging with therapy easier, and it's so hard that any small improvement is a good thing. The SSRI medications that we spoke about earlier are also an antidepressant, so they will help. Your support will help. Keeping going will help. Try not to allow your child to wallow; fresh air, distraction, company are the things they need, not solitude. Even though they'll object, you've got to persuade them out of their room.

When our son looks at his future, he has an image of himself still struggling with OCD, unable to leave the house, unable to have a career or a family. That's a really depressing picture. It'd be great if he could use that picture as motivation to fight OCD so that it doesn't happen, but it's so overwhelming that he sinks into depression and kind of accepts his fate.

If I consider that future, my brain just freezes. I cannot, and will not, accept that picture. He has so much potential, so much to give to the world, there is no way that OCD will rob him of that. If a sheer bloody minded refusal to accept that fate was a cure, OCD would be long gone already, but it isn't. All we can do is deal with each challenge as it presents itself and trust that, one day, we'll win. It has to happen, anything else is absolutely unthinkable. I am advised to be realistic, to consider his difficulties and modify my expectations but I won't. I have modified my expectations as much as I am prepared to. I accept that achieving the future he deserves is going to be hard. I accept that it's going to take much longer, and is much more complicated than for other children. And, that's as far as I'm going. There's the line. OCD will never cross it.

TIPS

* If you notice any symptoms of other conditions, speak to your doctor or therapist.

* If your child is suffering from depression, try not to allow them too much time alone. Try to engage them in activities that used to interest them, even if they're not very enthusiastic about it.

* Anorexia takes priority over all other symptoms. This is one problem that can carry severe health risks.

* Be patient. Sometimes a new obsession can just fade away as quickly as it developed.

* Watch for specific triggers, for example, make notes of when your child pulls hair and what's happened around that time. Often, there's no explanation but sometimes there is.

* Keep talking to your child about it – keep communication open.

So, if I know all of this, how come he's still suffering?

I know that everything I've said in this book is true.

I know that CBT with ERP works to overcome OCD. It has the best success rate; it is the medically preferred treatment. I know how to do it. I also know what makes OCD worse. I know all of these things and yet, our son is still suffering.

Why should you listen to me? If I'm so good, surely I should have effected a miraculous recovery in my own child. I should be able to sit here and tell you how he's now a straight A student, with a crowd of friends. I should be able to tell you that he's healthy and has never looked back. I should be able to tell you that his future is bright and all of these problems are behind him. I wish I could. There is one problem, though. One piece of the puzzle is missing and that piece is one I can do very little about. You see, I can't do it for him.

The sufferer has to choose to enter into ERP because it is so hard, the anxiety can be so brutal, they have to be totally dedicated to success. They must know that they will possibly feel worse in the short term, but the long-term benefit is worth it. They have to want to do it for themselves. Not for their parents, or their therapist, or to shut people up. They have to want to get better – at any price. Choosing to do an ERP task has to be their decision. They must feel as if they have some control. That can be very frustrating because they don't always make such great choices, since their choices are so influenced by OCD. But it is crucial that they don't feel forced into it. If you do try to force them, there is a strong probability that they won't do the ERP task fully, and that can leave them feeling as if they have failed, or they can even lose faith in the therapy, the therapist or you. Trust between you all has to be maintained because what they have to do is so scary for them. They have to have enough confidence in your knowledge and ability to do it even though it scares them.

Our son isn't there yet. He does want to get better but we are still waiting for him to find the strength and the willpower to stand up to OCD once and for all. We are waiting for the day when he walks into therapy and does all the exercises because he wants to. Right now, he tries but still avoids the anxiety whenever he can and sees therapy as something to dread because it makes him feel awful. He'd prefer not to do it, even though he knows he needs it to get better. We're closer than we were but we're still not there yet.

Until that day, all I can do is support him along the way. Learn all I can. Encourage him, support him and love him. It's my job to be on top of all the treatment options, to make sure he's getting the right kind of help at the right times, and follow up on those treatments at home, no matter how tough it is, how tired I am or how desperately our son fights against it. One day, he will find the strength he needs to go to battle and, when that day comes, I'll be ready.

I do hope that you have found some of my experiences useful and that my musings have been interesting for you. I wish you all the luck in the world. Stay strong, keep laughing and remember, you're doing a great job.

Thanks for listening.

OCD RESOURCES AND WEBSITES

UK
OCD UK

A good resource for information. OCD UK provide funding, organise small support groups around the UK and offer a helpline for you to call for advice, information and support for OCD sufferers, friends and carers.

Helpline: 0845 120 3778

Email: support@ocduk.org

Online: www.ocduk.org

OCD Action

A great source of information, they provide advocacy to assist in accessing treatment and to help deal with issues like discrimination, offer a helpline and a great online forum, run local support groups and offer great support handbooks for parents, sufferers and schools. Their OCD At School section is packed full of resources for schools, including lesson plans, advice and a forum for those involved in the education of young people with OCD. Invaluable.

Helpline: 0845 390 6232

Email: support@ocdaction.co.uk

Online: www.ocdaction.co.uk

OCD At School

Part of OCD Action, working directly with teachers to assist them in educating young people with OCD.

Online: http://school.ocdaction.org.uk/teachers/

USA
The International OCD Foundation

The one stop shop for OCD information in the USA! In depth information, guides to selecting the right therapist, even lists of recommended therapists and specialist treatment centres, local support groups and online support...definitely check this site out!

Online: http://www.ocfoundation.org

Beyond OCD

A small organisation with a big heart, this Chicago-based charity are a great source of information and support for sufferers, carers and professionals, including teachers and the clergy. Check out their downloadable guides, packed full of advice.

Phone: 773 661 9530

Online: www.beyondocd.org

CANADA
The Canadian OCD Network

Find your local support group and reading material.

Online: http://canadianocdnetwork.com

Australia

Anxiety Recovery Centre

Not OCD specific, but working with a range of anxiety disorders, the Anxiety Recovery Centre offer a helpline to offer advice, support and referral.

Helpline: 1300 269 438

Online: www.arcvic.org.au

Mental Health Association NSW

Here you can find a list of local support groups that aren't OCD specific, but are open to anyone with an anxiety disorder, including OCD.

Online: www.mentalhealth.asn.au/find-support/anxiety-support-groups. html

INDEX